To Millie with
best regards,
George E. Lee

George

A Hoghead's Random
Railroad Reminiscences

A Hoghead's Random Railroad Reminiscences

George E. Leu

VANTAGE PRESS
New York

Published by Vantage Press, Inc.
516 West 34th Street, New York, New York 10001

Manufactured in the United States of America
ISBN: 0-533-11331-8

Library of Congress Catalog No.: 94-90695

0 9 8 7 6 5 4 3 2 1

To the families of those engine and trainmen who worked in *pool freight unassigned service* and *extra boards*. They knew not where or when their breadwinner's next trip might be; and, to my wife, Doris, the woman who adapted so well to that lifestyle only to find her husband retired and spending days in the recreation room writing about it.

Contents

Acknowledgments

A number of people kept me from being derailed with a project that began as a grandad's recollections of his former occupation. I am grateful to the following:

Bruce Anthony and classmates at the Magnolia Community Center; Agnessa "Sisi" Larsen and classmates at Sisi's writer's critique class; North Seattle Community College Senior Adult Program; Halina Pawl for her all around help and her "you must put this word and that word in the glossary" advice to an old *hoghead* who assumed everybody understood our jargon; Mr. Warren W. Wing, for his generosity in allowing me to use the pictures that open each chapter and the many railroaders from all departments who encouraged me to continue the endeavor until these stories were in book form.

Introduction

Gheez! I thought. *This monster of a steam plant is on wheels!* Then engineer J. J. Murphy, a 1908 hire, shouted across the cab of the *Mallet** locomotive, "Get your damned beak out that window and watch ahead!"

The fireman reacted immediately. The words and the tone of voice made a lasting imnpression on me. I'd just turned twenty-one years old and was an observer on that trip in 1940. This newcomer had hitched a ride from the mountain town of Skykomish to Seattle, Washington. Hurrah! The Great Northern Railway had accepted my job application.

The engine had entered a curve to the left as the fireman explained the name and purpose of various valves and levers for my benefit. He'd made an obvious mistake by diverting his attention from the track. The reprimand came railroad style.

I had doubts. Would the work be steady? Wedding plans depended on that. Could I pass the physical and the

---

*Note: Railroad lingo or jargon words appear in italics the first time they are used in the text. They are defined in the Glossary.

Book of Rules exam? Did all locomotive engineers holler at firemen like that stern-looking guy had done? Would I get canned if I told one of them to go to hell?

A student fireman must make the required number of trips without compensation or meal and lodging allowances. It meant my meager savings must be tapped in order to continue. I'd better get going on this endeavoar because the first trip with pay would establish an all-important seniority date and influence future income.

My early indoctrination became a harbinger of things to come and of an interesting forty years ahead.

A Hoghead's Random
Railroad Reminiscences

Chapter One
The Little Giant

Great Northern Cascade Division engine crews anticipated a job loss upon completion of the eight-mile Cascade Tunnel plus line change and the electrification on the east slope. But they hadn't figured on the catastrophic Great Depression of 1929. That came as a second blow.

Paul Gustavson, a 1908 hire and Skykomish resident, had suffered with the furloughed enginemen. He described those bleak years accurately when he advised us, "Why . . . why ya needed twenty years of railroad seniority in order to hold a summer job—with the United States Forest Service."

Many years without a new hire created an unusual situation for newcomers. The age gap put us on the left side of a locomotive cab, working with men who'd begun their careers before and shortly after the turn of the century. The mostly patient veterans served as both train movers and instructors. They had a lot at stake and doubtless adopted the policy, "Better teach 'em right on this trip; I

1

might get stuck with one of 'em on another run." I considered that early introduction to railroading as on-the-job training or apprenticeship at its best. But for the first step in our training, we had to be examined on the "Consolidated Code of Operating Rules" by an official.

Veteran railroaders called him "the Little Giant." We knew of him as Mr. I. E. Clary, Interbay trainmaster. That "old guy" (anyone over fifty-five) might be tough. Some employees described him as a tyrant. He stood about five feet, eight inches on his tiptoes and was a little on the rolypoly side. The fellow appeared to be a giant to any employee not completely dedicated to the Great Northern Railway.

Clary strode into the room puffing on an old black pipe, took a seat at the head table, and slowly scanned his audience. I thought he doubted any of us would become capable railroaders. The legendary official had moved up from brakeman, conductor, and *snow king*. He also had survived the Wellington disaster of March 1, 1910, when an avalanche engulfed two passenger trains. Clary later became Cascade Division superintendent. He had a special interest in that young group in front of him; our mistakes might cost him some sleepless nights.

One droopy-eyed rookie had overslept and rushed in ten minutes late. The hapless hopeful compounded his problem several times when he corrected Clary on name pronunciation. The brazen one, not yet on the payroll and already running late, dared to *back into* the boss. The somber official took three slow puffs on his pipe, stared over his spectacles, and said, "Young man, before you and I are through railroading, I will have called you a lot of different names."

Charley Murphy, another 1940 aspirant, had cut a honeymoon short so as not to miss that all-important examination. We, the young bunch, naturally judged Charley's situation as a truly supreme railroader's sacrifice and certainty good reason for insufficient study of the rule book. Clary extended no sympathy, although a rare and fleeting smile indicated the stern-looking guy at the head table might be a different person behind a facade. The name Murphy may also have helped Charley.

At any rate, all present passed the first exam, its purpose being to evaluate the new hirees and establish the safety-first aspect of railroading. We would soon discover that a locomotive cab would be our real classroom.

Only old-timers and relatives dared call Clary by his first name, Ira. Relatives on the Cascade Division jokingly referred to themselves as "members of the royal family." Two brothers-in-law worked as trainmen on long hour local freight runs because of the big pay checks, but a large portion of their earnings supported two race horses. Their wives knew little about about the track, or of oats and stable expenses. They did know household money shortages existed. "That cheap GN railroad must surely be the reason. Our husbands worked long hours and should have received more money. Well, now! Ira is the superintendent. Certainly he can correct the injustice." Clary dreaded those numerous complaints. He knew of the monetary shortfall, but dared not divulge the reason. The phone calls continued. The Little Giant couldn't get that bothersome burden off his back.

Another brother-in-law, Engineer John Finn, a 1903 hire, solved the superintendent's problem. John worked trains 27 and 28, the fast mail. He came roaring across the Snohomish River flatland at eighty miles per hour one dark winter morning. Two horses suddenly appeared in the headlight's beam. John couldn't stop in time. Those horses would race no more. The chief dispatcher notified the superintendent of the reason for a delay to *Number 27*.

A dour-faced Clary came downstairs from his office in the King Street station to meet the now very late mail train. He greeted the engineer with typical Claryism when he said, "John, that's the first good thing you ever did for the family."

Clary, the former snow king, continued to worry about the *bill* each winter when the white stuff blanketed the mountains. He wanted no delays on his division. The snow-dozer conductor reported frequently to the boss by company phone. I became the subject of one conductor-to-superintendent conversation while working the job as a fireman.

We went on duty at 6:00 A.M. that bitter-cold Monday morning and completed a few chores around the Skykomish yard tracks. The job would then head ease to *big wing* Scenic, Berne, Merritt and Winton. But first, I needed to take water on engine 1246 from the main line spout. Conductor Bill Caughlin came out of the depot and shouted to me on the *tank top*, "Don't fill 'er up! Clary wants us to try the old water tank up at Alpine to make sure water is available there. The boss thinks this clear weather is just a break before the last 'big one' hits. He's worried about a dozer or rotary crew getting blocked between slides and running out of water."

We departed Skykomish believing Clary's idea a good one No one could remember when that water tank had been used last. Trees had grown up where a sawmill once stood. The door to the old depot hung ajar night and day during the several years I had passed the place on electric locomotives.

A problem developed as soon as we *spotted* for water at Alpine. A raised steel skirt had been welded on the old *tender* to adapt it to newer spouts. The modified tender and the ancient supply source appeared incompatible. The spout barely reached the intake on the tender, let alone fitting inside it. I decided to stand on the spout in order to hold it in position. I needed to pull hard on the chain and hold it down to open the supply valve, but didn't dare let loose until I could safely jump down to the top of the tank. The procedure didn't work—not on that first attempt.

A pull on the rusty old chain and some cursing failed to get results. I tried, tried again, and shivered on the precarious perch. Was the outlet valve frozen, plugged, or had the old reservoir gone dry? Suddenly, the water gushed out under great pressure. The spout kicked up, and my feet slipped off the icy metal. I twirled in the deluge, remembering: hang on to the chain regardless; wait for the exact time or you'll take an awful tumble off the tender.

My next try succeeded. With the tank full, I returned to the engine cab, my sodden clothes beginning to freeze. The conductor and crew had enjoyed the show. They thought it had been a great performance, especially when I stuttered, "Tell the superintendent there's water available at Alpine—lots of it."

The work must continue so I hung all my clothes on the *boiler head* to dry. We dropped the canvas rear-cab curtain, closed the left side window, and proceeded east. An embarassed fireman became almost comfortable—except when forced to lean out into a cold wind in order receive a brakeman's signal.

We took water again that afternoon at Merritt and went to *beans*. Conductor Bill returned from the phone with a message from the superintendent. I wondered, A compliment for my checking on the water supply at Alpine? Sympathy extended for the hardship endured? I should have known better. Clary's directive was, "Can't have young fellows running around naked on the mountain; looks bad for the railroad."

The Little Giant had a strong loyalty for the veteran railroaders he'd worked with during his days as the snow king. They'd endured tougher times before completion of the big tunnel. One fellow, we called him "Dutch," counted on Clary's loyalty in the years to follow. Dutch, a 1910 hire, had worked as the fireman on one of the dozer crews. He feared not when officials gathered to observe. The guy had a way with words, but one needed to listen carefully to understand them.

The superintendent surely remembered Dutch and a miserable winter day during the early 1920s. Multiple snowslides in the Cascades had tied up the railroad. The dozer engine sat between two of them: out of water, immobilized, and waiting to be rescued by another crew. A vice president, distraught over the traffic stoppage, waded through waist-high snow to the engine and shouted at Dutch, "Why can't you get off your butt and start shoveling some of this damned snow into the tank and make some water?"

Fireman Dutch, always a showman, went into his act. First came a careful tug and adjustment of his cap visor. Next, a cursory look at the surrounding snowdrifts before he said, "Mister, does ya know how much snow it's gonna take ta fill da tank?"

"I've no idea. You tell me."

Dutch readjusted his cap and this time used more than a minute to scan the area. He then pretended to be doing some serious mental mathematics before replying, "Hmm, dat's gonna take a hundred acres, about, hmm, eleven feet deep. Where ya want me to start?"

Dutch loved to use math—his special kind—to answer questions. Clary remembered a formal investigation concerning a collision between a work train and a local freight on the curve west of Halford. The interrogator asked, "How far did your locomotive move after you first saw the opposing engine?"

Dutch replied, "Eleven feet six and three-fourths inches."

"My God, man! How on earth could anyone be so accurate about distances at a time like that?" All present felt sure Dutch had hung himself with his too-precise figure.

"We was backing up. I saw da other engine and jumped. When I opened my eyes, dere it was right above my head, da back end of da left number two side rod. You think I would come here and lie about dat? Well, den you go to the *roundhouse*, find dat engine and measure dat distance."

Many years later, Dutch, now an engineer, sat facing his old conductor / snow king, now the superintendent. He'd counted on Clary to get him out of a jam several times before. This one would be more difficult; Dutch had been *on the bricks* for a year due to a serious rule violation.

A sharp dresser when the occasion warranted, Dutch wore a too-small fuchsia-colored jockey cap, a faded purple sweatshirt, and dungarees. All were spotted with light green paint, and his jaw bulged with a chaw of tobacco. He explained he'd just left his job as a busy interior decorator to attend the meeting. Aha! So *that* would be his strategy. The proud former employee did not intend to plead for a return to his previous occupation; it would be only as a favor to the Great Northern Railway.

The Little Giant puffed on the old black pipe and then opened with, "Dammit, Dutch! You always came in to see me before and made promises. Were you too ashamed this time because you kept on breaking them?"

Dutch replied, "No, sir! I makes a promise, den I keeps dat promise. You're looking at a guy who keeps his word."

The Little Giant evaluated the errant one's audacious approach. He abandoned any script or plan and began to give Dutch hell. Nothing promised or implied gave the culprit reason to be so confident. Reinstatement hadn't been mentioned, but he complimented the boss on the wisdom of putting him back to work. Clary continued to berate. Dutch, now calling the superintendent by his first name, said, "Ya sure made a good move, Ira." The spiel went on, "I've made dis company a lots of money, and now I can git out there and make 'em a lot more. Ya know I do a good job and don't cause no troubles."

A side door opened and another official entered in time to hear Dutch's last remark. The new arrival interjected with, "Well now, Dutch, that depends on what you consider trouble."

The show's second act began as Dutch evidently feared the new arrival might jeopardize his reinstatement. He arose, glowerd at his nemesis, and said, "No troubles means no brakeman's hurt or killed and no engines or cars busted up."

The newcomer and Dutch faced each other and moved around the room. The official, in full reverse, attempted to increase the distance between them. Dutch continued with, "Do ya know why dat is?" He proceeded to answer his own question as he placed a paint-stained finger to his forehead and said, "Dat's because dere's too . . . damn . . . much. . . up . . . dere."

The adversaries continued to circle the room as Clary observed. The more vehement Dutch's oratory, the more the tobacco juice sprayed. The official wore a new light tan suit and snappy necktie. He had good reason for backpedaling.

Dutch returned to work and and retired with dignity a few months later. Clary had done all he could for an old friend.

Clary specialized in caustic comments. A frequently errant conductor had been notified to appear for a formal investigation. The little giant insisted that he personally conduct this particular *butt burner.*

The culprit, the guest of honor—the one who hoped to beat the rap—hadn't arrived. A puzzled Clary inquired if all present had received the proper notification. They had, and the absent one's union representative arose and said, "This conductor is also a CPA. At this time of year he is very busy doing income tax returns for numerous clients."

Another person inquired, "What's a CPA?"

The Little Giant wasted no time answering that question, snarling, "In this case it means 'Continual Pain in the Ass.'"

A switch foreman had earned a spot near the top of Clary's "give 'em hell" list. The boss thought of him whenever things went wrong at Interbay Yard.

The Milwaukee Railroad used tugboats and barges to move traffic from the north, down Puget Sound and into Seattle. One stormy night several boxcars came loose and fell overboard. Clary noticed them bobbing offshore as he drove by on his way to work. Upon arriving at his downtown office he immediately called the Interbay general yardmaster and inquired if a certain switch foreman had worked the previous night.

He received a "No, sir, Mr. Clary, not last night."

9

"OK, I thought sure he had because I saw the boxcars floating in Elliot Bay this morning."

Sometimes for the sake of running a smooth, efficient railroad, the Little Giant found it necessary to discipline a stubbornly "by the book" employee. This requires real Clary strategy.

Clary ordered a trainmaster to escort the bothersome one to the office at a certain time. The brash brakeman faced the superintendent. "Young man," Clary began, "I've an important question to ask you."

"Why, yes, Mr. Clary, go right ahead."

"OK. Just when can we expect you to stop being such a horse's ass?"

"What's that? Errr . . . ah. . . ."

Instead of an expected reply, the Little Giant said, "That'll be all."

As he left the room the brakeman asked the trainmaster, "What's the superintendent so mad about?"

"I suppose it's because you didn't answer his question."

I sat opposite Clary one morning after being promoted and while working off the engineer's *extra board*. The notice for me to appear in his downtown office came as a surprise. I'd already been cleared of any wrongdoing by a formal investigation the previous week. My passing a red *mainte-nance-of-way flag* had caused the hubbub.

We'd rounded a curve with brakes already in emergency and found two extra-gangs at work with the rails up on jacks. The big Mallet slid to a stop only twenty feet before running out of railroad.

Clary sat at his desk, gave me a stony stare, and motioned that I sit down. "I've been reading this transcript," he said. "It's about your near-disaster west of Sultan. You say you got a *short flag*. How can you be so certain the distance between the yellow and the red flag was not the required one and one-fourth miles (changed in 1967 to two miles)? Those engines don't have speedometers, let alone odometers. Seems to me you were pretty damn careless when you entered that curve not under control." The Little Giant leaned back in his chair as if he held a good poker hand.

I replied, "Mr. Clary, I gave the roadmaster hell about the flag placement, and he said, 'Oh, it was about a mile.' I then complained about the red flag not being in plain sight, and he agreed that it would have been hard to see. I now know the exact distance between those flags."

"How can you be so sure?"

"Because I drove my automobile up there last Sunday. A gravel road parallels the railroad on the south side; I checked the distance on the odometer."

"Hmm." The superintendent leaned across the desk. "How far was it?"

"Eight-tenths of one mile."

"Are you dead sure of that?"

"Yes, sir."

Clary reached into a desk drawer, pulled out a piece of paper, and said, "Well now, the general manager is really hot about it. He wrote me this letter. Here is what he thinks. I'll read a part of it to you. 'This engineer is very young and inexperienced. I believe he, the fireman, and the two brakemen were carrying on a foolish conversation and failed to hear the *torpedoes* or note the warning flags.' Now you know how he feels about this."

I stood up and shouted, "Why that's the most stupid thing I've ever heard! Forget about the rules. All of us on the engine had a better reason for being alert. We had a heavy wheat *drag* and sure as hell didn't want to be on that Mallet if she rolled over and down a bank."

Remorse followed. One didn't pop off at an official who had been a railroader fourteen years before I was born. Would he hold a grudge? Clary arose and said, "The reason for your being here today is that we don't want you to get cocky or careless, because you were not disciplined following an investigation."

Later, I wondered why Clary hadn't handed me that letter to read. Was it a fake? Why hadn't that track been taken out of service by train order? Had someone else boo-booed, and must they be protected? Oh, well, I'd survived, been declared innocent, and remained on the payroll. Wait a minute! Where did the general manager get that "inexperienced" crap? That hurt as much as if I'd received a rules' violation penalty.

The Little Giant didn't win 'em all. One senior conductor had plagued Clary for years. They called him "Nap" because of his initials, N.A.P. His brakemen disagreed with that explanation for his name. They averred Nap was called Nap because that's what he did in the caboose all day while they busted their butts *shuffling boxes*. Give the guy credit: he skillfully avoided Clary's wrath time after time. Finally, the Little Giant would have his day. The boss pulled Nap out of service until he appeared for a formal investigation. This would be discipline at its best. It made no difference that both Clary and Nap were of the Catholic faith. The Little Giant intended to give him hell that morning. Younger officials must also attend. They'd learn a lot from this one.

Clary and his entourage sat waiting for the culprit. The boss puffed on the old black pipe as Nap entered. But a stranger accompanied him! Had he brought an unknown union representative? Nap approached the head table, and said, "Mr. Clary, I'd like you to meet my good friend, Father Corboy." The Little Giant's pipe fell to the floor as he stood up to greet the priest. Clary appeared at a loss for words—the ones he had intended to use that morning.

The boss appeared at his best during a *joint track* investigation held at Tacoma. A massive derailment had scattered thirty-five cars over both main lines—on a hillside, over a bridge, and a few went into Puget Sound. Who must pay for this "big one"? The Great Northern had spilled 'em, but the Northern Pacific maintained the track. Testimony established that the Great Northern had complied with all rules and train orders. It also appeared the derailment began on the bridge that was undergoing extensive repairs.

The Northern Pacific disagreed. They contended the first car had derailed fifty-five feet west of the west bridge abutment. Their witness testified he had climbed into the wreckage and made a careful study. The Little Giant challenged that statement. He had too much actual experience for the NP's witness, and it showed as the contest dragged on into the evening.

Clary focused on the impossibility of access into the wreckage and that no one could determine the exact point of derailment. He intended to prove his point by calling on one of his own employees, the derailed train's rear brakeman, Clarence Anderson. Clary inquired, "After your train came to an emergency stop, could you have gone forward to the *head end?*"

Anderson replied, "Yes, sir."

The boss hadn't expected that answer! Next question: "With car bodies, wheels, brake equipment, twisted rails, crossties and gravel, are you still of the opinion you could have made your way to the head end?"

13

"Yup."

"Come now, wouldn't that have been impossible?"

"Nope, a boathouse sat just over the bank from our caboose. I could've rented one and rowed around the mess."

Even the tired old interrogator had to smile. The need to take a water route to the head end proved that the wreckage could not have been carefully explored as testified. The Great Northern escaped from picking up the tab on that one—the Little Giant had done his work well.

Clary received an urgent message from the Spokane Division one afternoon. "Locomotive in *turntable* pit—the wrecker crane attempted to pull it from pit—crane also now in pit. Can you send the Interbay wrecker SAP?"

The Little Giant replied, "Not sure I should—do you have any more room in the pit?"

Clary never bestowed a direct compliment. On rare occasions one might be delivered via a third person. Section foreman John Micone had been assigned the onerous task of moving three buildings adjacent to the *back lead* at Skykomish. The job required they be moved out and around numerous telegraph and trolley wire poles.

John must have sought advice from loggers around the town. He had set up an intricate pattern of blocks and cables, while awaiting our arrival with engine 1246. The brakeman removed the *knuckle* from the rear *coupler* and replaced the *pin* through the cable loop. All buildings sat at new locations after only three hours and a dozen pulls.

The minimal time and cost to the company must have surprised the superintendent. He passed through Skykomish on the *rail-auto* a few days later. Some said the Little

14

Giant just wanted to see what he believed to be the impossible.

Did John the section foreman receive a well-earned compliment? Well, yes, but it came Clary style. Trainmaster Ed Carter delivered the message: "The boss said to tell you he had a damn good notion to have you put those buildings back where they came from just so he could see how you did it."

My group naturally relished the third person Clary quote: "Those damn kids sure fooled me. I thought I'd be up every other night when we promoted 'em. They turned out to be a good bunch of young *hogheads*."

I'd occasionally meet with the superintendent over union contract differences during those later years. My phone call and inquiry regarding an appointment always got the same answer "I've been busy since 1904, but come down here anyway."

The Olympic Hotel's main ballroom and balcony overflowed with railroaders at Clary's retirement party. The guest of honor said very little. He didn't need to, for he'd already said a lot and influenced many during his years on the Great Northern. The Little Giant had *coupled* the past to the present for all of us.

Chapter Two
Our Mentors

The two locomotives stood nose-to-nose and coupled together in front of the Skykomish depot that Fourth of July, 1937. The contestants, a Westinghouse *double-cab* Z-1 and a Mallet R-1, vied to shove the other in a reverse direction. Two wins out of three attempts would supposedly indicate the most powerful.

After two defeats, the Mallet's engineer demanded another chance. "She spun 'er wheels," he hollered. "The electric's quicker thrust did it, and I didn't want to chew up the rails. Give me enough time for steam to reach the cylinders, and I'll shove those two streetcars to hell 'n' gone down the track."

Pow! Pow! The Mallet's thunderous exhaust shook nearby buildings. Then both locomotives paused before the electrics gave ground and whistled, "Surrender. . . ." The crowd cheered although most realized the contest didn't really prove superiority. They enjoyed the show unaware that main line diesels waited in the wings to displace both of those old reliables.

16

Many familiar names on the engineer's seniority roster disappeared into the past. Some of them, as scoop-shovel firemen, had moved a mountain of coal into ever-greedy locomotive *fireboxes*. They'd endured long enough to run engines on trains such as the *Oriental Limited, Empire Builder, Western Star, Cascadian, Owl, Internationals,* and a variety of freight trains. Ah, yes, they'd handled the heraldic "silk trains" that raced across the country on a schedule, envied by today's railroaders. People hurried to trackside just to watch those *highballers* whiz by. Minutes, not hours, governed penalty payments for a failed on-time raw silk delivery.

Steamships hustled the valuable cargo of silk from Japan. Keith Frost, a 1937 GN hire, knew of silk trains before he became a railroader. He'd been at sea with the American Mail Line on runs from Yokohama to Seattle. Those ships steamed into Victoria, B.C., en route to Seattle. Longshoremen boarded there and immediately began opening hatches and loading pallet boards in advance preparation for their Seattle arrival. Some said, "Bales of raw silk moved shoreside and into railcars before the ship had finished docking."

Rayon, a new fabric, challenged the silk industry and won. The lucrative and exciting silk runs became history.

E. W. (Dad) Ross, a 1898 hire, had been a link with those glory days of railroading. All young kids on the beach along Puget Sound knew Dad as the engineer without the traditional shop cap, the one with a close-cropped haircut. He passed us every other late afternoon and always gave a hearty wave as he rattled by on *Number 5,* the westbound *Cascadian.*

Ten years later the Interbay crew caller stunned me with "You're called for *Number 2,* the *Empire Builder.* Ya

Last of the famed P-2 engines to leave Seattle. *The Seattle Times.*

better be down here early. Dad Ross expects his engine to be *oiled around* and ready to go." I questioned the call. Didn't a fireman need a year's experience to work in passenger service? "Take the call or else," he said. "There's no other firemen available."

It worried me. This engineer's regular fireman had been older then my real dad. I'd not tell him about my having been one of those kids on the beach a decade earlier. The old man might reply, "Young fella, I wish you were still there instead of on this run with me tonight."

His now gray-haired crew cut appeared just below the gangway as I washed the cab floor with the deckhose. He yelled and backed down and away from the engine. Wetting down my hoghead with hot water and steam could not be considered the best way to begin my first trip on a *highwheeler*. One knew Dad Ross would be boss on that engine, and yet he made that point without much fuss. However, I did receive a reprimand on this first trip.

Passenger trains in the electrified zone used a heater car to supply the train with steam heat. They housed an upright *fire tube* boiler and burned a high-grade diesel oil. I lacked experience on that equipment.

At first it appeared almost too easy. I hadn't heard any communication whistle signals from the conductor demanding more heat. I shut the thing down through the *Big Tunnel* to prevent fumes from entering the cars. I went back and fired 'er up again as we exited the east portal and returned to the cab rather pleased with myself. The heater car had a *full head of steam* and more than *half a glass of water*.

Dad greeted his, now cocksure fireman with, "Young fella, I'm sure glad you're with me tonight." I wanted to hear more—and I did. My hoghead continued, "The fire you have coming out of that heater-car stack is much better than any headlight. Why, I can see the trees, the mountains, the fields, the river. . . ."

It was the way he said it! I looked back: the fire extended up over the heater-car stack and formed a gigantic blowtorch, which brilliantly illuminated the area. If the train stopped or slowed, the concentrated flame might damage the trolley wire. Dad knew of the danger; another young fireman had done that very thing in front of the Wenatchee depot. The old man made his point with me, but appeared cool and matter-of-fact about it.

We returned the next day on the *Cascadian*. After *swapping power* at Skykomish and entering the lower valley, I noticed Dad reaching into his work grip for candy bars. He'd wave and toss them to kids along the way. I'd gotten to know him a little better by then and complained, "How come you never tossed candy to the kids at Carkeek Park and Golden Gardens when I waved at you in the early 1930s?"

As any good railroader should, a surprised E. W. "Dad" Ross had the answer. "Young fella, I always ran out of candy before we even got to Everett."

Al Strandrud, a 1903 hire, had lived at Tye (Wellington), during the early days of his career. Huckleberry picking and deer hunting served as diversions at that little railroad town located near the west portal of the old three-mile Cascade Tunnel. Other old-timers said the tall, wiry engineer had packed deer a mile out of the woods on his back unassisted.

We *lost the wire*, while descending the east slope on a trip with Al on *Number 28*. I argued with the stoic Scandinavian about what we should do with our inoperative air compressors. Shouldn't we stop? Dared we come down the hill with only the air in the reservoirs? Al listened, took a

Al Strandrud's last run (left to right): Bill Strandrud, fireman; Frank Crutchley, road foreman; Dick Tanguay, trainmaster; Bill Lowney, master mechanic; Reginald Whitman, superintendent; George Leu, union representative; Al Strandrud, engineer; Lee Barnes, trainmaster.

look at the gauges, and ended the conversation with ... "You yust might be right—but I don't tink so." Most old-timers would not have been as diplomatic with a brash young fireman.

After his retirement, Al made a journey to Wisconsin where he'd spent his childhood. The trip later turned into a disaster. On a street in Saint Paul, Minnesota, an out-of-control automobile struck the seventy-seven-year old former railroader. He returned to a Seattle hospital minus one leg and with the other badly injured. I visited Al one day during his long and painful recovery. I'd hoped to cheer him up a bit.

He appeared talkative and said, "I must tell you a story about myself as a young boy on the farm in Minnesota ven I got lost in a snowstorm. I knew our farm vas near a lake, but it got dark and I ended up on the wrong side of that lake. I saw a light and vent to a farmhouse. Those nice people said I should have supper and spend the night with their kids, and they'd take me home after breakfast the next morning."

Al smiled as I interrupted with, "Does the leg hurt a lot?"

"Ya, the one I got left does."

"I heard you have a good bone specialist on your case."

"Ya, he yust left the room."

"Oh, what did he have to say?"

"He said, 'Didn't you get lost in a Visconsin snowstorm about sixty-five years ago and spend the night at my parent's farm?' "

John Finn had followed his father from Ireland to a job on the Great Northern. Some said his dad, a section foreman, put son, John, on his crew payroll three months before the kid left the old sod. Both brought a boxcar load of Irish brogue and wit with them.

Young John left his dad's crew to become a locomotive fireman in 1903. Four years later after John's promotion to an engineer, it was necessary for a Section Foreman Finn to flag a train to a stop because of track repairs. The veteran engineer on the stopped train climbed down to congratulate the father on his son's recent promotion. The old man deflated any existing ego or status symbol the veteran hoghead might have had with, "Well, the kid was no good for da section, so I thought he might do a fine job running an engine."

In the mid 1920s John Finn traveled to Washington, D.C., to appear before a congressional committee on a national wage-rules dispute.

Management averred that engineers already enjoyed a most generous pay scale. It appeared management intended to use the young hoghead from the far west to prove their point.

"Mr. Finn," the railroad's representative inquired, "are you now employed as a locomotive engineer?"

"Yes, sir."

"Were you working in that capacity on the Great Northern's Cascade Division during the month of January?"

"Yes, sir."

"Now then, I have here copies of two pay checks issued in your name. Each is for a two-week period in that month. Would you please examine them, tell me if you received it, and if the amounts are correct?"

"Oh, yes, those were my checks all right."

"Mr. Finn! Each check is in excess of two hundred dollars! How is it possible for you to appear here and assert enginemen are not generously reimbursed for their service?"

"Well, in a way, those checks were easy money, because during that month I worked on the mountain in snow removal service I didn't have the bother of taking my shoes off at night and putting them on again in the morning."

"What do you mean?"

"There wasn't time for that; we stayed on the engine and plowed snow night and day. Oh, do you happen to have copies of my checks for the month of February?"

"No, I do not. Why do you ask?"

"Because I sat by the phone each day hoping to go out on a run. Yeah, February, a poor month—made only sixty bucks."

Management should have left that witness in the mountains out in that other Washington.

Mark "Punk" McLean acquired his nickname as a young lad who hung around the Interbay roundhouse before hiring out in 1905. He later earned another title by the way he handled a passenger train. Others said the "Slicker" had such finesse with the old H-6 brake valve that he could *graduate the release* to a point where a wee bit of sand on the rails stopped the *Empire Builder* at a station.

Not so on one predawn September morning in 1918. He rattled the cars with a hard stop on the coastline between Seattle and Everett. But then the muzzle of a train robber's revolver at his head gave reason for that rough stop. A bandit entered the locomotive cab via the tank top and fired one shot to show he meant business. He then ordered the fireman to uncouple behind the mail car. They then moved down the track a few miles.

The Miller River Bridge collapsed under his locomotive on another trip. Mark also survived a tragic mud slide, which dumped his engine into the Skykomish River near Monroe. The train crew managed to pull him from the almost submerged engine. The not-so-lucky fireman perished in the flood-swollen river.

I remembered yet another episode when an excited McLean brushed by me without a word as he ran to the Skykomish depot. As the night *hostler*, I could hardly wait to bring his power to the top end of the yard and back to the roundhouse. I hustled to the depot and asked Third Trick Operator Charley Eby, "What ailed that hoghead on *Number 4*?"

Charley said, "McLean wanted to have the dispatcher stop all eastbound trains at Monroe. He'd come around Applegate Curve above Index, and looked straight down from the end of the ties a hundred and fifty feet to the Skykomish River." The moniker "Punk" could well have been updated to "Rabbit Foot."

J. W. "Buck" Ewing, a 1905 hire, irritated some dispatchers because he'd stop his eastbound drag to take water at Halford. Others often took water at Gold Bar, while picking up a steam helper, but only if they thought 22,000 gallons wouldn't take the Mallet from Interbay to Skykomish. Not so with Buck. He'd stop his train at Halford, just eight miles west of where he would swap his power for electrics.

Short and stocky, Buck came equipped with a quick wit and a sharp tongue. He'd run out of water once between stations—"Ya can't make steam without it,"—and he'd never do that again.

The chief dispatcher's message, sent over the superintendant's signature, read, "Please advise this office why you must stop for water at Halford."

Buck's equally terse reply stated, "Find it difficult to take water at Halford without stopping."

Horace Parks and Frank Cushman both hired out in 1909; Frank in March and Horace in April. Their promotions came only seven days apart. The two highly respected engineers became close friends during those many years. Each tried to outdo the other as a prankster. Both, robust and in good health, labeled the other as an "old codger who should have retired long ago." Frank won the big one—call it his coup de grace.

Horace had eased his train to a stop upon arrival at Vancouver, B.C., on *Number 360*, the *International*. He grabbed his work grip and began to climb down amongst the many passengers on their way to the depot. There came a shout. Good friend Frank was rushing through the amazed crowd pushing an empty wheelchair to assist—the train's engineer!

We absorbed much of the needed train-handling methods from the veterans. Each had a certain skill and / or idiosyncrasy. Alert firemen, in that classroom on wheels, could pick and choose which mentor to emulate.

Another veteran engineer advised fireman Tom Elliot, a 1941 hire, "Ya don't learn much from the experts around here. It's from watching guys make mistakes; that's how ya get good at this business."

They worked a long hour local freight run for several weeks until a senior employee bumped the young fireman. Tom and his hoghead shook hands and said their farewells after that last trip together. Tom took a few steps, but returned to say, "Oh, and many thanks. You were right. I sure learned a lot from you. I couldn't have worked with a better guy to find out how to 'get good at this business.' "

One day the same engineer stood "on the carpet." Not the one in the superintendent's office; this time his wife conducted the investigation—at home in Skykomish—on a payday. She knew the checks had been delivered, but the cash on the kitchen table failed to meet her expectations. The tirade began: "Where's the rest of the money? I've talked with other engineers' wives, their husbands bring home much more than this."

We, who had fired for him, knew a card game Panquingui took a good chunk out of his paycheck. "Pan" served many rails as a time killer, while they awaited a work call at the distant terminal. They'd play for an hour or two and won or lost modest sums, but the game enthralled this guy. He'd "give the shirt off his back" to any needy person—just don't bother him at the Pan table. Night and day he sat there at both the home and away terminals, a cigarette dangling from his lip and one eye closed to avoid the smoke.

Give him credit; he knew how to duck trouble such as, "Where's the rest of the money from your paycheck?" He replied, "Can I help it if we hauled mostly empty cars for that two-week period?"

Absorbing the rudiments of railroading from many different people could not be avoided. Our idols rarely erred, and they suffered the most when they did. One such, an expert on troubleshooting electric locomotives, goofed in front of an audience. He'd been called to run *light engine* from Skykomish to Dryden with a *two unit* Westinghouse and help a westbound drag. His power hadn't been started. The engineer noted the small roundhouse crew at the depot to make the power change on *Number 6*, the *Cascadian*. No problem, he'd start 'em up. The passenger train departed, and the people at the depot, plus Electrical Superintendent

Joe Gaynor, saw the expert troubleshooter rushing towards them.

"Joe," he said, "that damned 5004 won't start. I've checked everything and she won't *take 'er bumps and come on line.*"

The offical pointed and replied, "Go back and lower the *pantographs*, have the hostler use a steam engine and pull you out of there and under the trolley wire. They should start OK." The embarassed expert turned and stared at the fully-extended pantographs searching the sky for a wire. The audience didn't ridicule; we thought about "familiarity breeds contempt" and other such warnings.

Earl "Kewpy" Smith, another 1909 hire, appeared as lean and nervous as a race horse. He ran his engine with a similar goal in mind. Competition existed on the busy joint track between Seattle and Portland. Crews from three other railroads vied to lead the pack so as to avoid being delayed en route. Getting over the road superseded polite protocol. Loyalty to the Great Northern inspired employees. So did the fact that an eight hour run paid the same amount as did the usual fourteen. That expedited trains as if it were a kick in the butt.

Fireman RJ "Bob" Smith, a 1940 hire, had already spent three years at the roundhouse. He knew railroad language, but this trip turned out to be postgraduate study.

GN *Number 671*, left Portland in good shape that morning. They'd picked up additional cars at both Lakeyard and Willbridge before hustling across the bridges to Vancouver, Washington, where they filled out to full tonnage. The GN local freight would hold and follow them out of there. Earl smiled; one obstacle already behind them. He envisioned the Union Pacific and Northern Pacific locals would be in on the *sidings* at either Castle Rock or Vader. The happy hoghead expected a straight shot to Centralia, the halfway point, and home in time for dinner.

Earl's first disappointment came with a message in the *hoop* at Kalama. It instructed 671's crew to pick up a car at Longview Junction; the *waybill* would be at Kelso just two miles beyond. That little ten-minute chore didn't disrupt Kewpy's plan for a speedy trip. Most conductors allowed the head end to get the waybill from the hoop without stopping the train. They'd send it to the caboose with the new *clearance* and train orders, while stopped for water at Centralia.

Not so with Conductor Sylvester "Steam Heat" Arnold. He'd walk ahead at the Junction, ride the engine to the Kelso depot, get the waybill himself, *roll the train by*, and catch the caboose, Kewpy fumed. The procedure required him to slow down passing by the depot, pull by with almost a mile of car, and slow down once again to pick up an old man with a crate of eggs speed. The hoghead shouted across the cab, "The old buzzard should stay in the *gorilla cage* where he belongs. His screwed-up way of doing things makes a thirty-minute job out of a simple one-car pickup."

The caboose moved by that depot faster than Steam Heat had expected. In fact, Fireman Bob surmised that if the conductor really did try to board with a crate of eggs there'd have been one hell of a mess at that depot. At any rate, Earl worked the throttle open and the old lumbering Q-2 went to work. But wait! The head brakeman looked back on the next curve and shouted, "*Hot box!* About ten cars back!" An utterly dejected hoghead brought the train to a stop. The brakeman gathered up the equipment and headed back to the trouble spot. Kewpy saw a beautiful run slipping away. Others might have accepted such a fate, but not this hoghead.

Bob noted that the conductor had left the caboose and headed forward. Did he intend to assist the brakemen working on that car? No, sir! The *skipper* strode by that hot box with barely a glance. A few minutes later Bob advised his engineer, "A man on the ground over here wants to speak with you."

Kewpy sauntered across the cab and looked down at his conductor. Steam Heat wasted no time and shouted, "Say, you poor excuse for a locomotive engineer, just where 'n' hell did you think you were going at Kelso without a conductor? I barely latched on to the caboose as it whizzed by. Both my arms were jerked out of their sockets."

Kewpy looked at the brakemen working on the hot box, studied his watch, and then replied, "Well, thanks to you, we've got lotsa time now. Come on up here and we'll shove those gawddamn arms back in place for ya."

Frank "Bluebarrel" Clemens came to the Cascade Division in 1909. He'd been promoted to engineer on another division, and had served in a supervisory capacity there. He may have taught us the most valuable and long-lasting lesson of all. He hadn't planned it that way.

Most young firemen considered that highballer an expert. We made remarks such as, "Wow! Only fifty minutes from Skykomish to Everett depot with a ninety-five-car train." Older, and perhaps wiser, railroaders witheld their praise. Most did agree the fellow with a big chaw of tobacco and cap visor turned up knew the trackage, and used it to the maximum mph. That speed often varied from the GN's posted *maximum permissable speed*.

As the day shift hostler at Skykomish, I'd often watched Bluebarrel come roaring into town. One morning, while on an engine's tank top, I saw Clemens rounding the curve west of town. The crossing whistle blasted away, while a loaded logging truck crept up on the tracks. The scenario took my breath away—if he broadsided that heavy load of logs they'd take out the depot and several wooden buildings across the street. The truck appeared to leap clear of the track with only inches to spare.

I climbed down and rushed to move Bluebarrel's electrics up the back lead so as to swap power. I wanted to let him know I'd witnessed the near-disaster and yet could be debonair about it. I greeted the veteran hoghead and said, "I thought we might need to clean bark chips and hunks of wood off the front of this Mallet before we sent 'er back to Interbay."

"Not this time, kid," he replied. "But I sure hope that gawddamn truck driver don't try that stunt again." Bluebarrel's only concern appeared to be a quick change of power and getting out of town. He reminded me of old movies featuring Pony Express riders changing horses and galloping away.

Bluebarrel placed a bid on trains 27/28, the fast mail. I'd not change power with him on those night trains unless 27 had been badly delayed. It came as an unwelcome surprise that morning in March, 1945. I noted the steam power for both 27 and *Number 3* sat on Maloney Spur. It meant more work on my busy twelve-hour-day shift. But why that crowd at the depot, and the five or six employees hovering around an automobile?

A hushed crowd inside the depot listened while Third Trick Operator Charlie Eby gave his phone report to the superintendent. "Yes," he said, "the fireman is dead and in the wreckage. Brakeman Kilde is in an auto outside with a badly mangled arm. They are about to leave for the hospital with him. The local engine is at the site. They will soon be coming down with Clemens and the remaining cars. No, sir, the track appears to be OK."

5011 in Foss River Canyon.

The local freight engine stopped in front of the depot. Bluebarrel stood in the gangway. I stared at his badly lacerated face. He looked from side to side as if hoping to locate the missing fireman. We moved towards the engine to help him down. Bluebarrel would have none of that, and took a firm grip on the *grab-irons*. He painfully inched himself down to the station platform. The once-proud and able expert ended his long career that morning.

No telltale wheel marks could be found on or near the point of derailment. The four hundred seven ton locomotive and one car must have separated from the train, sailed, and then plowed a path to a forest service road below. The experts figured locomotive GE 5011 rounded the east approach to Foss River Bridge at sixty-nine mph. The ten-degree curve had a posted speed of only twenty mph.

Other railroaders said, "I thought he'd be the last guy in the world to do that," or, "I'd 'ave bet my last dollar on him." The legend of Bluebarrel Clemens served as the lesson of Foss River Canyon. It educated all of us.

Chapter Three
Skills and Idiosyncrasies

The city of Skykomish sits in a narrow valley. The Great Northern Railway, the roundhouse, the river, and the town cuddle together there. All eastbound trains changed steam engines for electric power in the center of town. A reverse swap occurred with westbound traffic. Freight trains had an additional task; they'd *cut* helper locomotives in and out of the middle of trains because of the 2.2 percent mountain grade to the east.

Before railroad radios, whistle signals most often served as the method of communications between the head end and helper crews. The peaceful-appearing place nestled in the mountains often became a noisy little burg. The residents adjusted to the racket, and maybe too much so. Rudy Haney, a 1909 hire, knew all about locomotive whistle signals; but this day would be different. A relief engineer worked his turn. Rudy and his wife planned to drive their new Oldsmobile out of the valley and down to "clam digger country." They'd spend the day shopping in Everett.

City of Skykomish.

Rudy walked across the tracks to a storage garage, picked up the car, and drove towards his residence on the north side of town. Meanwhile, Ernie Wells, a 1912 hire, had traded his electric locomotives for a Mallet. He then eased westward on the back lead towards his drag on the main line.

To Rudy's credit, a large building obscured his view of the crossing, but the blasts from a Mallet's steam whistle certainly advertised its presence. At any rate, the Oldsmobile didn't look the same after being broadsided by engine 2041.

Ernie's accident report advised there were no casualties or injuries. It failed to mention the hurt of Rudy's pride, evidenced by his, "If I hadn't spent most of my life sitting under a damn steam whistle, I'd 'ave never got hit."

The town's nonrailroad residents only smiled about the "all-in-the-family" crossing accident. Not so with Trainmaster Ed Carter; he'd witnessed the collision from the depot platform. Ed knew that Rudy and Ernie had served as local union officers. He couldn't resist the opportunity, and said, "Well now, that's the first time I ever saw two union representatives get together on anything."

Engine crews on the other railroads knew us as the "Skykomish hunchbacks" even when away from our mountain habitat. We'd automatically bend low, and never, never raise the *tank hook* above a parallel position when taking fuel or water while atop a steam locomotive's tender. A $5/8$ inch wire carrying 11,500 volts sizzled overhead.

Bud Worthington, a 1941 hire, received an additional warning one night. He'd intended to fill engine 2502's *"Vanderbilt" tank*, while working as a night hostler. Bud barely beat the odds when he reached out with the steel rod to pull the spout around. Experts reasoned he had not actually touched the wire, but the rod had passed through the magnetic orb or field.

The jolt flung him about twenty feet and almost off the tank top to the ground below. The ordeal left imprints—the one in all our minds and the ones in the grime on that tank top. The blown-out shoe nails indicated where Bud had stood. He'd been *juiced* badly enough to have learned the names of all the nurses on his floor during the year he spent in a Seattle hospital.

The near-tragedy had a sequel. Bud returned home and walked to the depot as *Number 5*, the westbound *Cascadian*, arrived and changed power. Tall, rangy Carl Hemstrom, another 1941 hire, bounded up on the tank to check fuel and water. He stood erect, his head only inches from the wire! The fellow on the ground remembered; Bud carefully signaled Carl into a crouch.

I enjoyed my soujourn as a hostler at Skykomish. It allowed a fireman with meager seniority to work regular hours and be at home each night. Other advantages included a chance to *springboard* onto an open helper service *turn* or a *work-train* job based at "Sky." Ah! But another unanticipated benefit appeared whenever I changed steam power for electrics with eastbound freight engineers. They'd always ask that one question. "Who's my helper hoghead?" My answer caused a variety of facial expressions—grimaces, frowns, smiles, so-so looks, and was sometimes followed by an expletive.

Their reaction indicated the head end engineers did not consider all helper men equally adept. The guy in the middle of the train just might be the cause for a rough and miserable trip. Likewise, sometime helper engineers criticized the man *on the point*. I'd heard them say, "How can that guy up there find so much slack in one train?"

His fireman might add, "Yeah, I went back to fill out the *meter charts*, and he stretched 'em out with a jerk that knocked me right on my ass." I listened and learned while they rated their peers.

All freight engineers smiled when advised that Jake Beattiger, a 1905 hire, would be running the helper electrics. I wanted to work with him someday before I'd be forced to leave Skykomish and return to Seattle. Because of Adolf Hitler's antics in Europe, Uncle Sam's railroad traffic boomed. *Old head* firemen became engineers, and my chance to work with Jake came much sooner than expected.

Jake, already on that *triple cab* Westinghouse when I tossed up a *work grip*, inquired about my hill experience. No reason to lie—the old man would find out soon enough.

I explained that his expertise was well-known and my reason for *marking up* on the turn. My answer must have pleased Jake, because he said, "OK, ask any questions you like. After we *cut-out* at Dryden, I'll take time to go over just one circuit and its relays. If you learn something new each trip, that'll be fine."

He imparted many other tidbits of wisdom, such as the crooked pine tree east of Merritt. It served as an all-important landmark, and one of the secrets of Jake's skillful operation over undulating trackage. He continued with, "Always be shut off through the sag at Winton, begin to load 'er up again at the east end of the Tunnel where you gradually pick up your load in *regeneration*. But don't grab it all until the twelfth telegraph pole!" I understood why others appeared happy with the way Jake performed as their helper hoghead.

Our work often consisted of a series of short trips within one twenty-four-hour period, referred to as working in the *aggregate*. It meant irregular rest with a couple of doughnuts, a thermos of coffee, and two packs of cigarettes just in case. Jake, in his sixties, stayed alert in spite of that unusual lifestyle.

The GN had set up bunks in a small space behind the Dryden depot's waiting room. Other amenities consisted of a *caboose cushion* for each bunk, a small desk, one chair, and, of course, the dispatcher's phone. A large potbellied stove heated the waiting room and agent's office. A rickety outhouse at the east end of the building served as the restroom.

John Irving, the elderly agent / operator, worked days, the only shift at that little depot. Many of our stopovers there occurred around midnight when the place stood cold and dark. We'd fire up the old coal stove and drag the cushions from the backroom bunks to a place on the floor near the stove for a catnap. Ah, such luxury until interrupted by the dispatcher's call and his curt, "Drag west now leaving Wenatchee, better start up the power and be ready for 'em."

Old John greeted us on daytime arrivals. His head bobbed from side-to-side and the right hand quivered from many years of sending and receiving those dot / dash messages. He spoke with a distinct Scottish burr and enjoyed badgering young firemen—especially if they returned the fire. The old man's caustic barbs and bantering must have broken the monotony during his day alone in the little depot.

John greeted us from the depot platform one morning with the news we'd be going west within an hour. He looked towards our power and noticed an ugly splotch below one of the cab windows. Someone had thrown an apple that splattered and dried. It gave John his cue. "See that!" he shouted over the whine of our three units. "One of you young fellows partied all night, came to work, got vurra, vurra sick and threw up."

I studied the residue with mock seriousness and sorrow before replying, "No, John. That's all that's left of an operator / agent who stood too close to the track when he hooped up an order. Probably no one had bothered to report it. Old operators are a dime-a-dozen ya know."

We hurried back from the Dryden Cafe, grabbed our grips and headed towards the motors. Old John sat at his desk with head bobbing, chuckling, muttering. "Not even reported . . . dime a dozen . . ."

Skykomish helper crews considered a Dryden *turnaround* trip a good catch. A family-operated restaurant nearby made that run more pleasant. The owners resided upstairs above the cafe and knew when hungry enginemen had cut-out of a train.

A too-late arrival might find the place closed or about to lock up. But many times Denny, their son, his sister Katherine, or Denny's wife Mary would be at the door ready to open for those guys in overalls. Others told of being at Dryden on a holiday when they expected to go hungry, but didn't—they went upstairs and dined with the family.

Wedding bells rang for Al Abdo, a 1941 hire; he married Katherine. The marriage produced two sons who grew up and became—No! No!—not restaurant entrepreneurs, but hogheads.

Westbound freight trains arriving in Dryden cut in *helper* locomotives at the east end of the siding. The intricate, but efficient, maneuvering of locomotives and cars involved a cooperative effort between *swing brakemen* and helper firemen to ensure smooth transfer of that brakeman's work grip.

The routine procedure saw the swing brakeman, work grip in hand, alight from the head end locomotive as it passed the east switch. He set the work grip in the brush alongside the track. Then he made his way back to the middle of the train where he uncoupled the cars and signaled the head end to move forward to clear the siding. Next he'd open the switch so the helper power could move out of the siding towards the rear cars. He remained there to *line the switch* so the head end could back its cars onto the helper.

The helper fireman, already on the rear motor unit, coupled it to the rear cut of cars. While still on the ground, the helper fireman would locate the swing brakeman's grip in the brush and place it on the trailing locomotive unit. The routine teamwork expedited the train movement.

But one morning, while on helper fireman duty, I failed to cooperate and advised the brakeman, "Your *Book of Rules*, rain gear, and thermos bottle are still in the weeds where you left 'em."

"Why?" he asked. "Are you mad at me about something?"

"Nope. I started to reach for your grip, and thank God I heard the warning above the noise from our power. A big rattlesnake lay curled up against it."

I didn't worry about rattlesnakes at Dryden on another westbound helper trip. They wouldn't be around that bitter cold December 31st. That trip with Helper Engineer Ernie Wells taught me the benefit of composure.

We'd missed out on the New Year's Eve, but looked forward to a rare holiday at home. The heavy drag's head end electrics had entered the Cascade Tunnel's east portal and started downhill. The helper kept pushing on the uphill side with Ernie just beginning to ease off with our units. I studied my watch so as to be sure and shout "Happy New Year!" exactly at midnight.

Other words came out instead. Our three units *kicked out* with a bang. The sudden loss of power at that crucial point (half the train decending and half ascending) caused a *break into*. We lurched to a stop. I cursed again, grabbed my flashlight and started back. Ernie shouted, "Happy New Year! Be careful. There's still 11,500 volts at the trolley wire."

I found nothing wrong on the two trailing units, and met Ernie in the lead unit. He pointed to a section of small copper-pipe above and said, "See that little bit of frost on that joint? I'll bet a dime to a doughnut our control air is frozen up right there. Here, I brought a *fusee* along. Let's thaw the thing out."

In less than an hour, with the units restarted and train coupled together, we continued down the hill. I'd envisioned a fate which included several hours without cab heaters in zero degree weather. A wee bit of frost on a tiny little pipe over my head caused big trouble. I began the new year with more railroad wisdom.

A few years later, on September 19, 1944, Ernie's cool head prevented a disaster. He'd been called to handle the Thomas Dewey Presidential Campaign Special from Seattle to Portland. The train ran as the second section of *Number 402*, the southbound *Owl*.

A blockage on their main line caused both sections of the *Owl* to use the northbound track. They'd moved through the darkness without the benefit of *block signal* protection.

The rule required the two trains to be spaced no closer than ten minutes apart at stations. Ernie rounded a curve and saw the Owl's *marker lights*; she'd stopped at the Castle Rock depot. Ernie, with train in emergency, struck the train ahead resulting in one fatality and fifty-eight hurt.

Bad luck followed Ernie into October 19, 1947. He left Wenatchee with a heavy freight drag and rounded the curve at Olds Junction where the Wenatchee River joins the Columbia. He saw that huge hunk of rock and clay hurtling off the bank just fifty feet in front of Extra 5010 West. It tossed both head end units over onto their sides. Fifteen cars in the train jackknifed, some sliding into the river. A brakeman, on his first trip, chose the water as a better place and jumped from the rear locomotive unit. He sought another occupation immediately upon his return to Seattle.

I'd worked many trips in helper service with Ben Hansen, a 1909 hire. He appeared nervous as we departed Skykomish that night in the middle of an eastbound drag. But Ben fidgeted a lot on normal trips. The engineer on the point had very little mountain experience and that may have added to Ben's worry. The full-tonnage train moved up the *two-two* and through the big tunnel real nice. Our triple cabs, already traveling at a fast clip when we cleared the east portal, careened on the first curve. Ben cursed when forced to ease off in *regenerative braking* to avoid an *overload kickout*. The train's slack did not come back against our helper power, which indicated the three GE's on the point were not braking.

POW! Either the head end or caboose had *dumped the air* and we crunched to a stop. I waited and then looked over Ben's shoulder at the air gauges. "The air is coming back," I said. "Guess this train is all in one piece, huh, Ben?" Ben, nervously puffing on a cigarette he had failed to light, did not answer. Instead, he hurriedly arranged the power and *field exitation* levers for a *roll into braking* set up. The guy on the head end would not make another dive down the hill if Ben had his way.

Ben didn't have his way and couldn't slow 5,250 tons of freight train plus 621 tons of obviously ineffective head end units. The train sped around two curves, over a bridge, and POW!

We braced ourselves for the second emergency stop. My now-furious hoghead shouted, "That's it! You walk up there and tell that bozo we're not going to ride like this. I'll not let this train move until you give me a signal with a fusee."

After walking only a dozen car lengths on my trek to the head end, I heard the ominous sound of releasing brakes. Wheels began to turn. I didn't want to be left there,

Just west of Olds Junction, October 19, 1947.

and latched onto the side of a boxcar. The train's speed increased without the sound of dragging brakes. I wondered: Ben said he'd hold 'er until he got a signal. Is this one of those old-time runaways? If so, do I want to be hanging onto the side of this car? The train's acceleration allowed only seconds for a chance to alight safely. I hit the ground running hard to keep my balance. Ben whizzed by me, too busy to look out or see my flashlight. The caboose then rattled by, and a walk that started out to be fifty car lengths would now be five miles to the depot at Merritt.

I worried about the crew. Surely they made it around the curve just east of the Nason Creek Bridge; otherwise I would have heard the derailment noise. Oh, well, not too cold, downhill, and a full moon made for easy walking. A deer hunter's camp fire glowed far below. I moved to the north side of the track and out of sight—who would think anything but an animal might be strolling around up here at midnight?

They made it! I rounded the last curve and saw the caboose marker lights on the main line at Merritt. Gordy Daufney, a surprised rear brakeman, stood near the west switch to flag *Number 28*. He asked, "How did you get behind us? I know damn well you were on that helper power at Skykomish."

"Didn't like the ride so I got off. We do that now and then," I lied. "It's the best way to come down the hill at times."

Ben had tried to hold 'em and failed; it caused me to take a midnight walk. He apologized. It wasn't necessary. Two feet on the ground at that time suited me just fine. We learned from the experience. An expert with a slide rule advised, "The compressors on those three General Electrics pushed more air into the trainline than could be drawn off by a *full service* brake application on the helper motors."

The 11,500 volt trolley wire ended a short distance west of the west switch at Skykomish. A steam helper engine ran light twenty-one miles to Gold Bar to assist full-tonnage freights up that one percent grade. We looked forward to a "Gold Bar Turn" and the exhaust bark of old reliable steam engine 3238. It served as a respite from the whine of the electrics on our usual trips to the east side. Rolling out of bed about 2:00 A.M. drew no complaints—the round-trip generally took only four hours.

We'd departed "Sky" on the Gold Bar helper before dawn that morning. My engineer, Red Williams, a 1910 hire, didn't say much at that early hour, nor did Shirley Alyger, our elderly *pilot conductor*. While checking our fuel and water from the tank top, I'd noticed Shirley leave the depot and head towards the engine with our train orders. He also toted a gunny sack.

Upon arrival at Gold Bar we headed down the back *lead* and stopped opposite the depot. Shirley went across the yard tracks to learn the location of *Number 442*, the train we were to help. Red grabbed the oil can and climbed down. A few minutes later he stood below the cab window on my side hollering like a stuck pig, "Is this your cat I found behind the *pilot beam*?"

"Not mine, Red," I quickly replied. The look on his face and tone of voice made clear; it had better not be my cat.

"OK. It belongs to that gawddamn conductor. He's gonna turn it loose down here where it'll kill all the baby grouse and quail. Here—take this gunny sack and put the critter in one of the tank lockers. Tabby is going home with us."

We eased on down the lead and in on the east leg of the *wye* to turn the engine. Shirley took a long time out front before he *lined up* the switch. Both of us in the engine's cab knew a fruitless search for a cat had caused the delay. Next came the tough part: Shirley confronted me with pertinent questions about the whereabouts of a cat. He explained that it had become a nuisance, climbed up on the screen door, and yowled to be let in all day long. Shirley's wife also complained all day long. "Get rid of it!"

I understood our conductor's dilemma, but then a silent code-of-ethics required me to not betray a fellow engineman. I mumbled, "Well, yeah, I thought something fell off the front of the engine as we went into that dogleg curve at the west end of Reither." It appeared to appease Shirley for the moment.

The eastbound freight arrived and cut off the caboose *on the fly.* We backed onto it, coupled to the train, and departed. With Shirley now on the caboose, Red suggested I put the feline passenger in the seat box where it would be warm and more comfortable during its journey home.

At Skykomish, with the caboose *dropped* towards the train and *tacked on,* I climbed down to line up the switch for the roundhouse. While on the ground I hollered, "Hey, Red, ya wanta hand our passenger down; I can let the 'cat out of the bag' here."

"Hell, no!" he roared. "It'll have too far to walk."

Later, at the roundhouse, I held the sack while Red untied the string. The cat gave each of us a disdainful stare and streaked across the railroad yard. I shouted, "Look at that thing hurdle those rails! There goes Shirley up the sidewalk! The cat will beat him home! It's already on the screen door!"

Shirley plodded towards the porch, looked up and saw his nemesis. He stopped, looked our way, shook his fist and shouted. We couldn't hear him. He must have used some profanity. He had good reason.

I enjoyed working with engineer Rudy Haney. At times he too irked Conductor Shirley Alyger.

Rudy, a farm boy without a great deal of formal education, read many technical books. I admired his savvy. He could talk by the hour on basic math and often did. He might also lecture on geology, astronomy, and other subjects. Some may have considered his verbal forays to be "horn blowing."

We occasionally waited at Gold Bar fifteen to forty-five minutes for the arrival of the train we were to help. The dead time generally called for a gab session. The subject matter varied between politics, current events, or a mini *Book of Rules* exam wherein we tried to trap each other with a question. At other times, if called out on short rest, we'd cat nap. Not so with Rudy. He always had a subject and we were stuck with it.

One morning I'd *spotfired* the engine, dropped the canvas cab curtain, and closed my window. *Number 442*, the midnight drag, had departed Interbay late. Conductor Shirley, working in the aggregate, got comfortable on the rear seat box. There'd be at least an hour wait. Our watch check showed 3:00 A.M.

Rudy centered the reverse lever, opened the *cylinder cocks*, closed his cab window, looked our way and said, "Do either of you know the name of that star ahead and over Mount Index?"

Shirley squirmed and uttered an expletive. I shook my head as a negative answer. "Well, now," Rudy with his captive audience continued, "that's Mercury, and the one we see so clearly at times on the east side of the Cascades is Venus." We flunked our early morning astronomy test. Rudy then delved into celestial navigation by early day mariners.

Our tired conductor fumed. He'd miss out on those precious forty winks. The lecture also caused him to look less knowledgeable than the engineer. He didn't want that to happen—not while a young future hoghead observed.

The block signal behind us indicated the eastbound freight would arrive in ten minutes. Class dismissed! Our professor grabbed the oil can and left the cab to check the *guide cups*. With Rudy on the ground, Shirley exploded, "I'm wise to that guy! Did you notice he wouldn't let us change the topic?"

I replied, "Well, yeah. But he sure appears to be well versed on a lot of subjects."

Shirley snorted, "I can explain that too. The last thing he reads at night is all he will discuss in the morning. A few days ago I stood at the Sky depot when *Number 6* arrived. John Malony, the postmaster, wheeled the cart alongside the mail car. He had a bit of trouble with a heavy carton, and I noticed the recipient: R. HANEY, SKYKOMISH, WASHINGTON. Now listen to this! The sender's name, y-e-a-h, stamped all over it, read *Encyclopedia Britannica*. Now you make a guess which one those damn books he studied last night."

I couldn't consider Rudy as egotistical. He'd told me about a team of mules on the family farm down in Texas. He said, "Those mules had more intelligence than any railroader. Each day out in the field, exactly at twelve noon and 5:00 P.M., they'd slack back so we could *pull the pin*. Those mules wouldn't move until they were uncoupled from the wagon. Show me a hoghead with sense enough to do that."

Leo Clark, a 1912 hire, could get a lot out of engine 3238. The sharp sound of the exhaust advertised a strong rhythmic-induced draft. Shucks—I mean, Leo made my job easier the way he *hooked up* the reverse lever. He did worry me on one trip.

A heavy snow extended into the lower valley, and the snowdozer had made a couple of sashays west to Gold Bar. The pile of white stuff on each side of the track gave evidence they'd been there ahead of us. That unusual procedure turned out to be a blessing for Leo.

We'd turned the engine, coupled into a full-tonnage *Number 402*, made the air test and left. With the speedy departure, and the engine barking like a fox, I thought, Oh, boy, this would be a good one. My complacency ended while passing the rock wall a couple of miles east of Index. Leo scowled and shouted. I couldn't understand him because of the noise, but quickly scanned the water level glasses, steam gauge, and color at the *stack*.

All appeared OK, so I crossed the cab and said, "What's wrong, Leo? Everything looks great to me."

The poor guy had trouble all right. He shouted over the din, "Not with me it ain't! I sneezed and my upper teeth are back there in the snow someplace. I looked your way in order to get a landmark on that cliff. Gotta drive down here when we get in. Maybe I'll find the damn things."

Leo found his choppers! They hadn't been damaged, thanks to the fresh snow and a newly plowed soft landing place. Good hogheads do *too* get rewarded!

I learned something each day, both on the road and in the roundhouse, from an assorted bunch of guys. That type of apprenticeship had many benefits ranging from how to change out a *grease celler* on a Mallet to taking down a broken pantograph and securing the *hot cable* on top of an electric locomotive. It came in handy in the years ahead.

I enjoyed those days, but knew it wouldn't last. Only four or five years seniority in Great Northern engine service gave me little choice where assignments and schedules were concerned. It was late 1944. The U.S. Navy had alerted me to have toothbrush and razor ready.

Chapter Four
From the Other Side of the Cab

Either Uncle Sam or the railroad stood ready to separate me from my family. Bucks in the bank had become most important. I wanted that hostling job in Skykomish and *bid on it.* The rail traffic boom had created a manpower shortage and forced the Great Northern to change the assignments from three eight-hour shirts to two twelve-hour stints. How wonderful—four hours of overtime pay, seven days a week, and my workplace just two blocks from home. Being home each night eliminated hotel and meal expenses.

Charley Brockman, a 1937 hire, also bid on and received the coveted 7 A.M. to 7 P.M. job. I envied Charley's seniority but not for long. He soon received a notice to appear in Seattle for promotion to locomotive engineer. I congratulated Charley and gleefully pounced on the vacated assignment.

George Gairns, a 1941 hire, assumed my former status. He hoped that I, too, might soon receive one of those "come to Seattle" letters. He didn't wait long. My notice read,

"You will prepare for examinations for promotion to locomotive engineer. Examinations to begin March 10, 1945, and will include operating rules, machinery, fuel economy, and the general rules of the Mechanical Department of the Great Northern Railway." It meant I'd be low man on an extra board once again. The new status took me away from home and family in Skykomish and into a rented room in Seattle. The rent would continue even though I'd often reside at other points on the Cascade Division.

Examinations came first. General Roundhouse Foreman Bill Blum conducted the air-brake portion. He'd been an air-brake specialist and an army sergeant during World War One. Bill had another specialty—profanity. "Reverently profane" best portrayed him. His descriptive words flowed freely most often, but when mad, he spoke as if he were a polite English language major.

One oral examination included the question, "Describe the procedure for on the road emergency repairs in case of a broken equalizer reservoir pipe." Charley Murphy, another 1940 hire, and I had discussed the problem earlier and sought help from Joe Brock, the expert at the roundhouse *air bench*. Joe assured us that we shouldn't attempt that repair on the road: "Not enough time or tools."

Armed with an expert's opinion, we made plans. If either received the question he'd give the book answer. The other would then inquire as to its feasibility. It happened! Charley gave the book answer, and I inquired, "How could anyone get in around all that piping in order to remove the plug?"

Bill, now on the receiving end, shouted, "What's that?"

"Well, you know the kind of tools we have on an engine."

"Lemee see . . ." Bill had all the information in his head, but reached for the manual, found the page and began to read, "Take exhaust service discharge plug from. . . ."

Next came the shouted, "Why the silly son of a bitch who wrote this crap! There ain't room enough in there for two gnats to have intercourse."

Another nervous future engineer handled a question OK—well, almost. It dealt with emergency repairs following a broken trainline brake pipe between engine and tender. It also gave cause for another lecture by our unusual examiner.

Bill said, "That's good, but ya forgot the most important part. You'd test that hook-up before ya moved the train, wouldn't ya?"

"Oh, sure, why of course I would."

"I believe ya, but then let me tell ya a story on myself when this thing actually happened. They called me out one night to ride a board of directors train with Engineer John Finn. The worried local officials were all over that train for fear something might happen with all the big brass aboard. Well, it sure as hell did, at 3:00 A.M., right out here at Carkeek Park. A busted trainline pipe behind the engine stopped us cold.

"Oh, I knew what to do all right, and I did it. But there I was between the engine and tank with six of those *long overcoat* guys holding lanterns and flashlights up my ass—damn hard to think things over." Bill exaggerated about those six lanterns, flashlights, and their location. I encountered a couple of them at times and never *that* close.

Eight women manifest clerks worked in an outer office behind a glass partition. Their typewriters could be heard from where we sat. Suddenly all became quiet in the other room. I turned my head. The women had listened to Bill.

Some sat with heads bent over on the typewriter keys to control their laughter. They must have thought, "So, that's the way they talk to each other in that big red building called the roundhouse."

I met Bill on the platform at King Street Station one late afternoon during the Christmas holiday season. He waited to meet a teenage son. The train arrived and people began disembarking from several points. Bill, obviously excited, kept a close watch, and then rushed towards one group shouting, "Son! Son! Over here—over here! By gawd you were sure easy to find; I just looked for the homeliest bastard to get off that train and there you were." Bill grabbed and hugged the embarrassed young man. One could tell he really thought a lot of that kid.

The roundhouse crew called Bill "Bull Moose." He rarely had to prove himself. A group of young employees tested him one day. They intimated that he was, well, maybe, over the hill and not as tough as he would have them believe. Bill bellowed, "You young punks keep that up and I'm going to stuff one of you and your smart-ass talk right through that open window over there."

The brazen bunch continued to heckle. They doubted the boss's ability to carry out the threat. Jim Finn, son of Engineer John Finn, retired as a senior conductor many years later. He remembered well that day in the mid–1930s when he found himself sitting in the gravel outside the roundhouse office window.

I came to know the Bull Moose better while in Seattle as a young extra-board engineer. One conversation related to a near disaster while westbound with a hill drag. "Bill," I said, "here's my locomotive inspection report. The 2041 is out there with flat spots on all wheels, both engines, I had to slide that Mallet more than a hundred feet."

The dispatcher clamored for the same engine to go east, so Bill immediately notified the wheel shop about the needed repair job while I waited for an expected tirade. Swiveling his chair around at the desk and facing me, Bill said, "Well, you're the first son of a bitch who flattened wheels and then came in and admitted it."

Young hogheads considered themselves on trial and some may have felt they must impress their elders. The locomotive inspection form or "work report" appeared to be a logical way to exhibit expertise. However, a full page of faults, either real or imaginary, created more work for busy roundhouse employees and their vitriolic general foreman.

One young hoghead did it again. A lengthy list of problems lay on Bill's desk. Bill noted the form, the signature, and rushed out to greet his nemesis. "You're just the guy I want to see," he said. "I've got some damn good advice to give ya about running one of those fugitives from a scrap pile. Now when ya hear a lot of pounding, rattling, and banging just keep going; ya got a good engine. On the other hand, when she sounds nice and quiet, like a sewing machine, ya sure as hell better stop and look'er over real good. Ya probably lost something off that engine and might end up in a ditch."

Another hoghead appeared to have illusions of grandeur when conversing with employees of a lesser pay scale. Bill overheard the fellow bawling out an *oil boy* because the engine had been improperly supplied. The roundhouse boss hollered, "Cut out that bullshit. You engineers are a dime a dozen, but oil boys are hard to find. Treat 'em nice or they might up and quit."

"Equal Opportunity" and "Civil Rights" had become very important during Bill Blum's later years as roundhouse boss. The hiring edicts handed down from top management had not been a problem for "Bull Moose"; he didn't change his mannerisms one bit. A person of a minority race was no different from an Irish, Swede, Pole, Scotch, or German working at Interbay—Bill berated them all. They saw through the rough exterior of a person with a genuine interest and concern for all employees.

The first black employee had been on the job several weeks when Bill said, "If there's any more of you guys and they're as good as you are, send 'em down and I'll hire 'em," and he did. One, a machinist helper, acquired a cut over his eye and had placed a white bandage over it. Bill noticed it from a distance. Bull Moose roared, "Hey! We've got another 'safety first' drive going on over the whole damn system. Gheez! People can see that white patch on your black noggin from a mile away. Go get some black electrician's tape and cover it."

Bill made periodic visits to the roundhouse long after his retirement—just to check on old friends. One wonders about the language he used after he died and entered the "Pearly Gates." He surely must have gone that route.

Bill Blum had a counterpart in the South End Interbay yardmaster. We called him "Old Man Shasky" and sometimes other names. He, too, had a rough exterior and a way with words. They'd most often be shouted and accompanied by a wild waving of arms. The guy'd charge out of his office giving what we termed his "airplane signals." The expression described his flailing arms, which resembled a spinning propeller. Other comments might be, "Old Shasky is ready for take-off over there," or, "Some day he will wind up and fly away to the top of Queen Anne Hill."

Shasky always managed to get the work done and a little bit more. "High-strung and truly dedicated" best described him. We didn't really dislike the guy. Our purpose was to contribute an honest day's work. We did complain about the one-more-chore before taking a lunch break or a late departure to the downtown interchange with the cars for other railroads. I suppose our being half-mad at Shasky all day made the monotonous *shunting* job a bit more interesting.

He charged out of his office at the end of our shift one late afternoon. Yup, one more task before *tie-up*. We'd need to use the main line and must hustle because a Vancouver, B.C., bound *international* would soon depart King Street station. Failure to make the move ahead of the *varnish* meant fifteen minutes of overtime pay. This yardmaster would have none of that; no sir, not Shasky. It might blemish his near perfect record.

A crew member lined up our route to the main line well in advance, and we swished by the yard office. Shasky stood in the doorway with watch in hand and a smile on his face. He'd done it again, one last chore and the engine at the roundhouse ahead of the *flyer*.

But wait! The switchman on the ground at the *crossovers* faced the engine and gave a *washout signal*. We lurched to a stop as the man on the ground pointed to the reason. A frantic mamma duck and her brood had two problems. They'd attempted to cross the railroad yard to a swamp on the east side. The little ones scrambled and tumbled over the smaller rails, but found the mainline steel insurmountable.

A hungry raven loomed as problem number two. It stalked the group and appeared to be making a dinner selection as if from a menu. The flock's frantic leader had to decide whether to go back and chase away the predator or continue to assist the ones up front. The dilemma appeared to be more than one mother duck could handle. To hell with Shasky! We rushed from the engine on a rescue mission.

The duckling-shuttle-delivery service had just begun when we heard the roar. Shasky came charging towards us shouting, and giving, yeah, his airplane signals. He began, "Don't you dummies ever look at your timecards. Dammit, I wanted the engine in the clear at the roundhouse ahead of the passenger train. Geeze! All this fooling around . . ." The old man became silent—no need to explain for he'd seen the reason. Next came more subdued orders from the yardmaster, already on his knees scooping up one of the flock. "Hurry up! Grab the little one over there or it'll be a goner for sure."

A disappointed raven flew to a perch on a wire-mesh fence where it watched an intended meal disappear in the cattails. We waited to follow the *hot shot* while smiling Mr. Shasky headed back to the yard office.

I'd worked into Vancouver, B.C., as a fireman a few times and knew a little bit about the industrial track layout. Now as a hoghead off the Interbay extra board, I dreaded that first call to work a midnight *goat* at that location.

It happened and a nervous young *runner* left the old Ivanhoe Hotel headed for the depot in a dense fog. I met the job's regular fireman and registered out. A stranger appeared while we inspected and prepared the old A-9 engine. He handed me the clearance with train orders and said, "If you're the hogger, we'll take this bloody machine and buzz off down the track. My name is Aleck Upton. There's three of us Uptons ya know."

I didn't know that and a lot of other things about working a switch engine in Vancouver, B.C. Another switchman climbed into the cab, took several fusees from the rack, and stuffed them in his back pocket. It served as my cue and I said, "Yeah, you'll need those to take care of me in this rotten fog. I could get lost up here on a day job in July."

"Aw, this ain't bad, mate," he said. "You'll be able to see my fusee signals about ten- or twelve-car lengths. There's been times when we've used police whistles to pass signals. One bad night a few years back, some kids were out here and they, too, had whistles. We had one hell of a night—couldn't tell who kept giving those bloody signals."

A long and loud crossing whistle qualified as an error that foggy night. I knew of the city street ahead but I didn't know of those bedroom windows located alongside the track. The standard two long blasts, a short, and a long, sounded strange. I winced as I realized that the noise from that steam-whistle's 2:00 A.M. "wake-up call" was reverberating off the building. My remorse did not erase the fact that a Yankee hoghead had damaged international relations.

The comradery with switch crews in B.C. helped assuage the hurt from a net pay loss because of heavy away-from-home expenses. "Yanks" and the "Canucks" often used the brief lunch break to kid each other about nationality or craft. I'd told a ribald story one night while at beans in the shanty near the Burrard Inlet dock. The fictional episode degraded switchmen. I thought it topped 'em all, and started back to the engine, but Switch Foreman Les Mundy hollered, "Now just a minute! After that last story, I've got to tell one about hogheads.

"Three Vancouver switchmen traveled to Mexico and attended the bullfights. All those present eagerly awaited the advertised highlight, a contest between a most ferocious bull and a famous Spanish matador. Alas, a delay occurred followed by a blaring announcement over the public address system: 'Ladies and gentlemen, the great matador for the main event is ill. Unless a capable replacement can be located the contest will be cancelled. Are there any in the arena?'

"One of the vacationing switchmen jumped to his feet. Did he have the needed special skill and bravery, or was it the tequila? At any rate, the substitute matador / switchman appeared on the field of combat dressed in a matador's finery.

"The bull snorted, pawed the ground, lowered its head, and charged his tormenter. The switchman feared not; his regular occupation had him facing oncoming locomotives. He'd merely stepped up on the 'footboard' as the engine rushed towards him. He found bullfighting to be a similar type of maneuver.

"The substitute matador stood his ground with impunity, and then quickly stepped up on the bull's head, walked across its back, and alighted from the other end. The crowd shouted, 'Ole!' each time the agile stranger escaped those dangerous horns. They loved this brave but unorthodox bullfighter. The frustrated bull paused and did a very nasty thing. Bovines often did this out in a pasture, but certainly not before thousands of people in a prestigous bull ring.

"Ah! But, the ever-alert switchman-turned-matador noticed the bull had taken time out and the reason. He rushed to the public-address booth and announced, 'Ladies and gentlemen, there will be a brief intermission: my engineer just fell out of the cab.' "

Switch engine jobs in Vancouver generally meant a ten-day stint. The added expenses caused two of those in one month to be a paycheck disaster. In the meantime, and between switch engine jobs at other points, we waited for the "big one": a call to return home and work out of Skykomish in helper-engine service. Those calls appeared to be rare, until after—why of course—our growing family moved to Seattle.

Occasional runs, such as the Rockport Local, known as the "upriver job" taught basic railroading, paid dental bills, and put new tires on the old jalopy. We'd depart Burlington and highball to Sedro-Woolley, a distance of only five miles. After switching every track in town, we'd move to the next town. The roundtrip to Rockport and back consumed fifteen hours and fifty-five minutes. A federal law caused the precise on-duty figure. A full sixteen hours required a minimum of ten hours off duty, which caused a late start the next morning, and many angry shippers. The crew cooperated, the business people were pleased, and a bountiful payday made us happy. Call it a coveted "daylight job," which began and ended in darkness.

The upriver job serviced Sedro-Wolley again on the return trip which gave rise to an oft-repeated story. "The train with its carloads of logs, lumber, shingles, and cement stopped east of town. The caboose stood adjacent to the grounds of the state mental hospital. The rear brakeman went back to afford flag protection against a log train. An elderly inmate had observed the local during his regular walks within the enclosure. He came to the fence one evening and asked the brakeman, 'What time do you fellows go to work?'

" 'Six A.M.' the tired brakeman muttered.

" 'Hmm, and what time do you quit?'

" 'Ten P.M.'

" 'Hmm, and how many days a week do you do this?'

" 'Six.'

"The old man scratched his head and said, 'Well, it appears to me you guys are on the wrong side of this fence.' "

Crazy or not, money-hungry extra board hogheads loved the job as we did another sixteen-hour bonanza, the Anacortes Local. It ran west out of Burlington.

The *Annie job* locomotive served as our link with the past. The old F-1 class engine had been sold for scrap, repurchased and placed back in service during the World War Two emergency. Built in 1892, the engine had a Johnson bar instead of a power-reverse lever. The five-foot, hard-to-move lever saw lots of action each day as we switched the city's industries before and after the trip to the big lumber mill at Shannon Point. One old-timer offered his advice on how to handle a Johnson bar. He said, "Now ya don't want to pick up and move all that gear out there six hundred times a day with brute strength. No, sir! Make sure there's no steam beyond the throttle working against ya: don't let the big-bar know you're going to move it; sneak up on the thing and throw it over real quick. Oh, and another thing, never anticipate the next move and reverse the lever before ya get a signal. Those damn' brakemen will cross ya up every time and want to go the other way."

He'd spoken the truth. Towards the end of a long day I augmented his instructions with some profanity.

Some of the logs hauled to Burlington by the upriver job went west to Anacortes the next morning. Mitchell Boom, a log-dump operation, often became the local's first stop. Logs could only be dumped during a medium to high tide in that shallow saltwater bay. A boommaster sometimes referred to a low tide as, "Not enough water here to baptise a bastard." In such cases the conductor must decide whether to wait for the tide or *set out* the cars and return to dump at a later time.

On one occasion, Conductor Jim Finn deemed it best to wait on the incoming tide. They backed their train onto a long trestle spanning a tideland. The crew couldn't resist the temptation; the low tide and sandy beach enticed them.

A clam digging expedition proved fruitful, that is until Trainmaster Ed Carter drove by in a company auto. Ed saw the crew returning with their bountiful harvest. He rushed to the scene and demanded the shellfish be returned to their natural habitat. The tide came in, the logs got dumped, and Conductor Jim summarized the event with: "Any damn fool knows if you can dig clams then you sure as hell can't dump logs."

We considered *pool freight* runs in joint track territory to Portland a good catch off the extra board. Those trains were numbered: first 672, second 672, and third 672. We called them the south end highballs. They moved at a good clip in the *double track* area—when not clearing passenger trains, standing behind other freight trains, *picking up* or setting out cars, and *taking water*. A good run took twelve hours, but the average on duty time varied between twelve and sixteen hours. *Young runners* adjudged those trips exciting, competitive, and they paid well.

The jargon word *highball* caused trouble for one regular fireman on the south end. The telephone company threatened to cut off his all-important contact with the crew-caller. Why? he demanded to know. The reason appeared justifiable. Others on his two-party line believed him to be an alcoholic, who received numerous middle-of-the-night calls "to come down for a highball."

Lucky young hogheads might also catch a troop train off the extra board. Those speedy runs paid the freight rate. They also served as ego-builders for us extra board engineers. We thought about the future when we'd regularly run one of those high-wheeled P-2 beauties.

Jack Murphy, a 1940 hire, picked up his phone to hear the crew caller say, "Troop train south for 9:00 P.M." Later that night he spotted the engine for water at the Centralia Depot. The fireman went atop the tender and the young-looking twenty-seven-year-old runner climbed down to oil around and make an inspection. A much older Northern Pacific trainmaster pointed his flashlight at Jack and asked, "Where's your hoghead, kid?"

"That's me," Jack replied.

"Kind of young to be running one of these 'high-wheelers' down here, ain'tcha?"

"Nope, there's a bronze plaque up there on the boiler head that reads: 'Maximum Speed of This Engine 79 MPH.' It doesn't say a damn thing about having to be that old to run it."

I'd assumed the *highcar* would be an interesting job. Its crew maintained the electrified area between Skykomish and Wenatchee. Line boss Harry Root, four linemen, a conductor, and an engineer called Leavenworth, Washington, home. The crew generally worked a basic day, but could be called out at any hour in case of a emergency. Winter snowslides, avalanches or any other trouble with the all-important trolley wire had them on the way, day or night.

My call had me *dead heading* on *Number 28* which arrived Leavenworth at 2:00 A.M. The depot thermometer read five degrees as I hitched a ride to town with the mail-sacks delivery.

There she sat on the *spur track*, a work shop on wheels with a wing plow stuck on the front end. I tossed my work grip up and climbed aboard. An oil stove, one bunk plus a caboose cushion caught my eye. I wasn't that inexperienced, and slept quite well among a conglomeration of tools and equipment. In a few hours I'd be the first patron at a restaurant across the highway.

Things looked much better after breakfast. I'd just checked lube oil, water, and filled grease cups on the three

Highcar.

Cummings diesels when Lloyd Duranim, the job's regular hoghead, boarded the highcar. He immediately unscrewed each grease cup to see if they'd been properly filled. Lloyd then moved around the power plant as if he were a mother-in-law looking for dust on window sills. His parting shot came after he turned off several engine-room lights, "You young fellows have been spoilt working under that 11,500-volt wire. Just remember ya don't have Coulee Dam backing ya up on this baby. No, sir, when your batteries are dead, then you're dead, and that's one hell of a fix to be in." I knew that the cab heaters depended on "Lloyd's Baby" having 'er engines running. But why had the old man laid off then waded through the snow at 6:00 A.M. to check on me?

With Lloyd's advice and tips from the linemen, I began to enjoy my winter sojourn on the highcar. Bill Haugh, one of the linemen, told me his in-laws had a sleeping room for rent just a short walk from the highcar spur. The price, one dollar and fifty cents, fit my road expense budget quite well. I'd soon miss the chance to sleep in that comfortable bed.

We made several trips out of Leavenworth for routine maintenance, but topped off the diesel fuel tank each night before tying up—just in case. A heavy snowfall blanketed the Cascades, and a warm Chinook wind might really mess things up for the Great Northern.

A knock on the door came at 5:30 A.M. with a shouted, "Big slide at Scenic! SAP call!" With the highcar running and a full crew, we hustled up to the depot for a clearance and train orders before highballing to the west portal of the Cascade Tunnel.

A wall of packed snow and debris blocked our route. Probing with long wooden poles for a missing avalanche watchman became our immediate but unsuccessful ordeal.

His body appeared several weeks later. He'd attempted to seek protection inside the tunnel but failed. Meanwhile line boss Harry assessed the amount of downed trolley wire.

Because of the narrow valley, this avalanche could not fan out at the end of its run. Instead it stacked everything to a great depth over the main line. Removing the mammoth pile with available equipment would be a challenge. We backed out of the tunnel and down to Meritt, so Spokane rotary plows could tackle the job.

Three old steam-powered relics came west, but each went east again to be repaired. They'd cleared slides and snow drifts for decades, but this time a solid wall, higher than their hood and *big wheel*, rebuffed their assaults.

A huge plume-cloud drew our attention while we waited at Meritt; it served as a locator for another gigantic avalanche to the north of us. Powerful field glasses allowed me to view the awesome sight as it plowed down a canyon at the east end of Round Mountain. I watched large trees being tossed up like ships cresting an ocean wave, going out of sight only to appear again at lower elevations. Because of the distance, I couldn't hear the tremendous din, which surely accompanied this granddaddy of all avalanches. It appeared to move in slow motion. The phenomenon affected no towns, railroads or highways. The Supreme Architect's massive recycling event did, however, affect one young railroader—it enthralled me.

Meanwhile, ingenuity prevailed at the first avalanche. A modern bulldozer climbed atop the blockade. It shoved the material down into a trough where a rotary's spinning blades tossed it out. Our tired and impatient crew took a position atop the highcar for their performance.

Linemen Bill, Tex, Oscar, and Harvey put on a super show above, while Harry carefully studied a thermometer and chart. It was his job to determine the correct tension

Rotary snow dozer at work, Scenic, Washington. *The Seattle Times.*

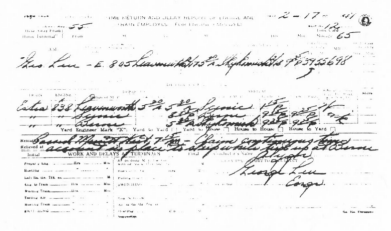

Time slip for on-highcar duty tour.

on the trolley wire to allow for the expansion and contraction of the line caused by seasonal temperatures. I moved the highcar in response to bell signals. My reactions had better be prompt; four tired, cold, wet, and hungry guys said so by the authoritative sound of that bell.

A weary bunch tied-up at Skykomish that night, and returned to Leavenworth the next day. I understood Old Lloyd's concern a week earlier. He must have known his relief hoghead might go forty plus hours on one of those SAP calls. He needn't have worried about his beloved highcar. I returned it in good shape.

Chapter Five
Investigations, Reasons, Alibis

"Ass-deep" described the snowfall on both sides of the mountain that trip in January 1946. I'd caught an eighteen-car troop train east. The colonel in charge asked if he could ride the electric locomotive from Skykomish to Wenatchee. The army officer got an insight on winter railroading in the Cascades that evening.

A brakeman flagged us to a stop at the east end of Merritt, and advised that the snowdozer had derailed up ahead. Our guest fidgeted and studied his watch. Ten minutes later Ted Micone, the dozer conductor, waded through the snow and boarded our power. He explained they had already *rerailed* the plow and would soon shove into the passing track and let us go. I introduced Ted to the colonel and we chatted for another ten minutes until the dozer cleared the main line.

Upon departing Merritt the army officer remarked, "I've been assigned to ride many troop trains, and you're the first engineer who didn't complain about a delay. A few really got hostile and cussed out the other crew."

I explained, "Railroaders try and stay out of trouble, and that conductor's wife happens to be my wife's sister. How'd I do for staying out of trouble that time?"

Sid Pierce, another snowdozer conductor, also had many relatives on the GN: dad, brother, brother-in-law, son, and a nephew. Paul Gustavson, the engineer on the job, pretended to have an "abiding faith" in his conductor that morning. At least it served as an alibi for a poor showing in a footrace.

The job's regular routine had been changed by a sizeable snowslide a short distance east of the Cascade Tunnel. The night crew now had the dozer behind the engine and couldn't shove through the slide on their way to Merritt, the crew change point. Because of the unexpected slide, the Seattle dispatcher arranged for another engine to transport Sid's relief crew to the blockade. They'd hike over the trouble spot and relieve the night crew.

Long-legged Sid broke trail and led the group to within sight of the stranded crew. Engineer Paul, the senior member on the relief group, brought up the rear. His age and time spent on a locomotive seat box had not prepared him for that kind of an ordeal. He wheezed and puffed as he slogged away some thirty yards behind the rest.

There came an ominous lull—a blast of wind—a brakeman shouted, "Avalanche!" The young and not-so-young ran for their lives.

The big one roared down from high on Rock Mountain, covered U.S. Highway 2, filled Nason Creek Canyon, and stopped several feet short of the railroad. Paul, with legs that could run no more, might have been engulfed in the swirling mass. True to his craft, he had an immediate alibi for his lack of speed. He said, "I could've run a lot faster, but then I saw our conductor kneeling in the snow with head bowed. With Sid praying for us, I knew we'd all be saved."

Conductor Sid declined credit for saving the crew. He explained, "Yeah, I ran right out of one overshoe back there. I tried to find it—paid twelve bucks for the pair at Maloney's store just yesterday."

Enginemen didn't have a monopoly on alibis. Conductor Dave Fox used words sparingly—as if he might run out of them before a debate could be chalked up as a win. He'd smile, hesitate, study his opponent through thick glasses, and then reply. His carefully selected words tended to disarm the other person.

We had arrived Wenatchee on an afternoon drag and registered in at the yard office. The trainmaster appeared, and announced he would conduct a watch test. We all knew that Rule Number Three required us to carry a watch, which "conforms to the requirements of the employing railroad," and "must present their watches to officers and supervisors for comparison upon request." All of us passed the test—except the skipper. Dave wore a three-dollar wristwatch.

The trainmaster shouted, "You call that thing a standard timepiece! Where is your railroad watch?"

Dave replied, "It's in my work grip out in the locker room. The second hand came off. I haven't had time to get it fixed."

"And just when did this happen, yesterday, last week, last month, or last year?"

"As a matter-of-fact, just this morning as we pulled out of Interbay yard. I rolled the train by me, checking the cars against my list. A piece of lumber sticking out of a car hit me across the chest and knocked me down. Hmm . . . I'll bet that's when I hurt my leg! Do you think I should make out a 245 form before I leave here? I'd sure hate to stick the Cascade Division with another reportable injury."

"You can go to hell!" the official said as he stormed out the door. But . . . but hadn't the trainmaster just violated rule 701 which prohibited "profane or vulgar" language?

Conductor Shirley Alyger had served the GN as an official during earlier days. He'd listened to many alibis and had come up with some dandies of his own. I'd wondered how he would handle one unique but embarassing situation.

World War Two rail traffic made it difficult to take train employees from their jobs at outlying points to attend a *Book of Rules* examination. But the Federal Law must be complied with. A bulletin advised that an impromptu exam would be held for operating employees in the mountain area. The class would convene in the Skykomish public library.

A mixed group of overall-clad people appeared for the makeshift exam. The area trainmaster would ask the questions and advise a stenographer how to score the answer. There would be no base hits, only home runs or strikeouts.

The testing moved right along, the company wanted us out of there and back to work in a hurry. We'd also be getting paid for this nonproductive time.

"Mr. Alyger," the examiner quoted, "on a train stopped under conditions in which it may be overtaken by another train, what would you do to afford full protection for your train?"

The old conductor had flagged more trains than most people had seen. Ah! But there had been a change to the well-known Rule 99. A hushed group saw a negative signal given to the steno. Shirley arose and demanded, "How could you possibly call that an error?"

The examiner explained, "Shirley, that rule has been modified. We can't go by an old rule and memories of how we used to do things around here."

The senior railroader in that room, still on his feet, and not about to be embarrassed, shouted, "Hold on there! You asked me how *I would flag a train*, and I told you. Now then, if you want a dishonest answer, rephrase the question."

Protecting a train's rear end had been stressed since before the Casey Jones episode in the early days of railroading. All operating employees knew Rule 99 would be a main topic during a rules exam—and that it consisted of eleven paragraphs. The practice continued with few changes long after Uncle Sam required *automatic black signal systems* on all main line trackage. Therefore, the rule became the basis for yet another often-repeated and, no doubt, fictitious story.

"An overly zealous trainmaster interrogated a student who did well on the quiz. But, the official pressed on with a hypothetical question: 'You are the flagman on a train that has stopped suddenly. The caboose is in the middle of a sharp curve. It's a terrible night with high winds and heavy rainfall. You grab your lantern, the flagging equipment cannister, and rush back to protect your train. But you stumble, lose the torpedoes and your lantern goes out. The whistle on an oncoming train can be heard. The engine's rapid exhaust indicates a high rate of speed. Your attempt to light a fusee fails; they're too wet. Now young man, tell me, what action would you take?'

" 'Golly, sir! I'd hurry and find a phone.'

" 'Good God! How would you find a phone out there in the darkened wilderness, and who would you call if you found one?'

" 'Oh, I'd call my brother.'

" 'And just who might your brother be—the dispatcher?'

" 'Naw, my brother don't work for no railroad, sir.'

" 'Hmm, then please tell me, why would you go call him?'

" 'Well, you see, my brother is real interested in trains. I'd tell him to git right down there if he wanted to see the damnedest train wreck he'd ever see.' "

Part of a dreaded, appear-for-investigation notice read: "To determine facts and place responsibility." It also listed which rules had, allegedly, been violated. Most often the superintendent already had reason enough to suspend or discharge the culprit. As one remorseful engineman described his situation, "Thirty days hath September, April, June, November, and one hell of a lot more days without a pay hath I."

The required five-day advance notice of an investigation appeared to be ample for some to concoct ingenious alibis. One superintendent asked an obvious rule-violator the routine question, "Could you have done anything to prevent the accident?"

The culprit replied, "Yes, sir, I could have laid off and not gone out on that run."

In 1942, Del Driggers came topside on a destroyer in the South Pacific just in time to take a ricocheted Japanese bullet to the chest. He returned to Seattle after spending a year in a naval hospital. Del married the girl of his dreams and landed a job as a locomotive fireman with the manpower-short GN.

A telephone call interrupted their honeymoon plans. The crew clerk gave Del the message. "Dead head on Number 4 to Skykomish for helper service." Del demurred and attempted to explain his dilemma. The crew caller had heard 'em all, and gave the ultimatum: "Don'tcha know there's a war going on? You're the only rested fireman available. Take this call or else."

The former sailor knew a lot about a war in progress. It had almost ended his life and delayed his honeymoon plans long enough. Both Del and his bride boarded the train at King Street station. Upon arrival at Skykomish, they checked in and learned he would not go on duty until late afternoon. Wonderful! The couple walked hand in hand across the street to the Skykomish Hotel.

Robert Burns said it first with his, "The best plans of mice and men . . ." But the GN had trouble on the east side of the hill. The dispatcher put out an SAP call for two helper crews, one to dead head and one to *double head* on *Number 28*. The hostler and his helper rushed to get a two-unit Westinghouse started and coupled to 28's GE locomotive.

Meanwhile, Roundhouse Night Foreman Joe Joyce headed over to town to call the engine crews. He ran into difficulty with the new fireman in the hotel's room 307. The guy didn't respond to the numerous shouts and door-knocking in an attempt to notify him of the emergency call to work.

Joe found it necessary to contact the hotel owner, who unlocked the door. Joe rushed in, turned on the light, and shouted, "SAP call to *double head* 28. They'll be in town in twenty minutes, so ya better get going." Oops, two people occupied that bed. A man's voice using understandable words ordered Joe from the room. Trains apparently failed to interest the ex-navy man at that time.

Joe managed to scrounge up another fireman, but the "fast mail" departed Skykomish thirty-five minutes late. The word spread: "A new fireman refused his call and stuck *Number 28*—there'll be hell to pay for that stunt."

A now rueful Del received his out-of-service-pending-investigation notice as he entered the roundhouse office. The regulars in town advised, "Ya just quit. Ya haven't got ninety days in. Hell, they don't even need to hold an investigation to fire ya. You'll have lots of time now to get caught up on whatever made you do such a stupid thing. But go to the butt-burning session, and show up there on time."

The investigation opened in the depot's waiting room. The trainmaster read the applicable rules, which had allegedly been violated. Joe, as the first witness, testified as to the culprit's blunt refusal to accept his call to work. Before others presented their testimony, Del's representative requested a fifteen-minute recess for a discussion with the trainmaster and first witness.

The three cenferred in a far corner of the freighthouse. The trio, given all the facts, agreed that extenuating circumstances certainly existed. A returned war hero deserved a break. The more they discussed the situation, the more heroic Del had been as a sailor in the South Pacific. The trainmaster agreed to phone Superintendent Clary in Seattle who OK'd a special disciplinary strategy.

Upon return to the waiting room to continue interrogation, the representative inquired, "Mr. Joyce, regarding your previous testimony in that you entered a hotel room, and notified Fireman Driggers to go on duty SAP; are you absolutely sure the person in that bed was the fireman sitting over there?"

"Well, no. He *is* a new employee I'd never seen before. The room number given me could have been in error. It's possible that I may have entered the wrong room."

The trainmaster immediately followed with, "If there are no further questions, I will close this investigation."

77

Surprise! A red-faced Del stood up. He had a question: "Mr. Joyce, how can you sit there and say you didn't barge into my room, turn on the light and holler, 'SAP call to double head *Number 28*'?"

A stunned group stared at Del in disbelief—sure, honesty is the best policy, but. . . .

The trainmaster said, "Lucky for you, young man, that this investigation closed before you made that last statement. However, remain in your seat. I will return in a few minutes and explain a few things about your job and the rule book you recently received."

Bill Leu, a 1948 hire and also a navy veteran of World War Two, had served on a ship, which rests on the bottom of the Coral Sea. This fireman's mistake occurred upon the arrival of train Number 2 at Skykomish. It also involved an important rule: insubordination. Similarity ended there, Bill's action amounted to an overly zealous application of Rule 709: the regulation that prohibited unauthorized persons from riding GN equipment.

Upon arrival and changing steam for electric power, Bill who was an extra board fireman rushed back to check the diesel oil–fired heater car and supply system for the train. A stranger in nonrailroad garb stood facing the boiler. He turned and said, "Hello, I'm Joe Gaynor." His attitude implied everybody already knew him.

This fireman would have none of that, and surmised a hobo wanted a warm place to ride. With an authoritative voice, Bill pointed to the open side door and said, "I don't give a damn who you are. Now get your ass off this car."

The stranger disembarked and disappeared into the darkness. The train left town as Bill filled out the meter chart and went to the head end. The guy he had evicted stood in the cab. Engineer Al Strandrud said, "Bill, meet Mr. Joe Gaynor, our Electrical Superintendent."

If the incident could be classified as insubordination, Joe wanted more of them. He'd enjoyed it.

A relief remote-control operator worked at Edmonds depot the night a train ran through and tore up the switch at the west end. The investigation began with the usual preliminary questions, such as age, length of service, and when last examined on the *Book of Rules*. All present remained relaxed, expecting a fervent, "Yes, sir" to indicate the operator's acceptance of the *little black book* as the railroader's law. Some yawned, others jotted down notes while they waited for the nitty-gritty to begin. They all knew General Rule A in the book left no doubt; its edicts went unchallenged.

The conducting official droned on with, "And do you believe in, and perform your duties in complete compliance with all applicable rules in the *Book of Rules?*"

The operator snapped all to attention with, "Now that's a good question. Some rules are ok, but there are others I sure don't agree with."

A five-day advance notice must precede all formal investigations. But the time period did not begin *until the date a rule violation became known to a supervisory officer.* A what-they-don't-know-won't-hurt-'em policy might be an errant employee's escape route. "Hush 'er up" then became the plan.

We called the conductor "Dusty," and the inquest pertained to an accident while his crew switched at Longview junction. The interrogation went quite well considering they had shoved a *cut of cars* into a supposedly empty track and messed things up. The superintendent prepared to close. The jittery crew could return home and sweat out a verdict, which might be fired, furloughed, or forgiven.

Dusty had to answer one final question: "Are your brakemen competent, do they follow your instructions, and perform their duties safely?"

The conductor replied, "Yes, they're a pretty good bunch of young fellows and don't cause much trouble." Satisfied, the superintendent attempted to close the investigation, but Dusty continued with, "Oh, there was that sideswipe in the Tacoma Yard, and the time we derailed three cars at Rocky Point. That's about it, except for a couple of weeks ago when we ran through the *tail track* switch at Vancouver."

Dusty had done it again!

Long overcoats had a thankless job. They made periodic tests for rule violations. Crewmen on passing trains often warned each other when roadside tests were in progress. The easily understood signal consisted of an open hand drawn across the knees in a sawlike motion—meaning: "Their coats were down to here—you're gonna get tested."

Norm Monson, a 1928 hire, did not receive a long overcoat advance warning. He had departed both Seattle and Tacoma late and planned to be on time at Centralia, the halfway point, on his passenger run to Portland. It should not be a problem, but Norm hadn't figured on two Northern Pacific rules-test people, who had selected a Great Northern hoghead as their prey. They felt certain their task would deliver a culprit, and set up shop in a woodsy area known as Wabash.

Bang! Bang! Two torpedos exploded seconds apart as *Number 562* rattled around a curve. Norm made an immediate speed reduction. Both he and the fireman looked for a fusee or flagman. Instead, they saw a portly gentleman standing to the right of the track—he wore a long overcoat.

A formal investigation commenced three days later. The alleged rule violation: "Excessive speed vicinity milepost 92." The test team averred the engineer should have slowed his speed to sixty mph but had reduced it to only seventy-three.

They explained two torpedoes had been placed two hundred feet apart on the inside rail before moving to a point where a path angled into the brush. One person, with a stopwatch, positioned himself thirty feet down the trail. The other stood at trackside, listened for the explosion of each torpedo, and signaled his partner when to start and stop the timer.

"Simple mathematics," he said. "The elapsed time between explosions as shown by the stopwatch indicated feet per second. That figure, easily changed to miles per hour, turned out to be 73."

The official conducting the investigation began the closing proceedings with, "Are there any further questions of these two gentlemen?"

A representative asked, "May we see the tape used to measure the distance between the torpedos?"

"No, we didn't use a tape. We stepped off the two hundred feet."

"Hmm, about your shoe size—oh, that's too technical. But about your hearing aid; when did you last have it tested?"

"I don't remember."

To the gentlemen who read the stopwatch: "About your thick eye glasses; have you had recent surgery?"

"Yeah, cataract removals."

"About the stopwatch: is it required to be of an approved make such as all railroad watches?"

"No, it's a French make."

"When did you have it cleaned and inspected?"

"I don't know. I bought it secondhand."

"Regarding other strict requirements of your railroad—"

The conducting officer interrupted with, "That's enough of that kind of questioning. The investigation is cancelled."

Another passenger train's hoghead represented himself before a general manager. The conductor forgot to inform him of a speedometer, a beautiful polished-brass thing, mounted in the last car—a private car—the general manager's. This hoghead also *took the blanket off* the iron horse in order to come in on time.

Upon arrival the official rushed to the head end shouting, "Just how fast did you go on that fifty-five mile per hour track back there?"

The man in the cab replied, "Why, er, ah, right on the money, yup, fifty-five is what we were doing."

"Well now, that's strange because my speedometer showed almost seventy. Explain that to me if you can."

"Hmm, yes sir, that is strange—I sure didn't see ya go by me anyplace."

Another freight train highballer used the "A good offense is the best defense" strategy. He had hustled downgrade on a division where a highway paralleled the GN's main line near the home terminal. The old timer had the Mallet *wound up* on the last leg of his trip.

Thirty minutes later at the roundhouse, a young trainmaster entered the room and began a tirade. "You did sixty miles per hour on the hill just west of town. You know that area is posted at only fifty for freight trains."

The old-timer finished his work at the register book, and replied, "Now, what makes you think I'd do a thing like that?"

"Because I paced you from the highway, that's how."

"I didn't see a company car on the highway this morning."

"That's because I drove my own car."

"What! Your own car! You don't mean that old blue Chevy?"

"That's right."

"Let's get this straight, we're talking about the one in the parking lot with a crumpled right front fender and in need of a paint job?"

"Yes."

"My gawd man! If you drove *that* thing over forty miles per hour, why—why, they should put you in jail."

Charlie Jensen, a 1909 hire, usually brushed off his critics when they complained of his "too slow" speed between Tacoma and Vancouver, Washington, in joint track territory. His mainline local freight run used fifteen hours and fifty-five minutes every trip. Charlie accepted his fate, and the big paychecks that went with the job. He'd adopted the two-speed system, slow and slower.

The Northern Pacific operated the trackage and were unhappy with the GN hoghead's method. They sent a train-master who demanded an explanation.

"It's this *turkey trail* railroad ya got down here," Charlie said. "There's too many curves."

The trainmaster countered, "Don't give me that baloney. We've clocked this train, and you're not running at posted speed on the straight track. Explain that to me—if you can."

"Sure, I've worked on this wooden axle railroad of yours for a long time, and I ain't seen any straight track yet that didn't have a curve on both ends."

A passenger train engineer on the same railroad had a much better reason for a late arrival at a depot. He calmly faced his heckler and said, "I'd rather be late at this station than on time into the river back there."

The required and faithful twenty-one-jewel standard watch plus mileposts served as speed indicators in earlier days. Glances at the reliable old timepiece and then translating the elapsed time into miles per hour had been the routine procedure. At slow speed on the mountain, one might use rail lengths in the same manner.

Electrical Superintendent Joe Gaynor surprised us one afternoon with a more sophisticated method. Sure the substation charts disclosed where and how fast his Westinghouse and GE's came down the hill, but an old Mallet had been used in helper service due to an electric locomotive shortage. We'd assisted four westbound drags, Merrit to Berne, and were cleared to run light, Merritt to Wenatchee.

On arrival we met Joe in the yard office. It appeared he had a reason for being there. He said, "Nice trip down the hill today. You did forty-five on the curves, but fudged a bit on the straight track." It baffled us. Didn't the expert know we'd brought an old steamer into town? It had nothing to do with the 11,500 volt hot wire or his substation charts.

Joe relished this type of scientific surprise and explained, "Those two big air pumps, mounted high on the *smoke box,* told me what I wanted to know. Each time you passed under an *air gap,* in the trolley, the exhaust steam caused a little blip on the charts. That and the exact distance between gaps served as a perfect stool pigeon."

Soon all concerned knew of speed violations out on the road as they occurred. Centralized traffic control, speed tapes, radar guns, and other innovations exposed blatant violations. Out the window went the admonition of the one old-timer who advised, "When the telegraph poles began to look like teeth in a fine-tooth comb, ya better slow 'er down a bit."

Vito reigned supreme as the crossing watchman at Galer Street. Rule violations, investigations, and discipline didn't worry him. He'd given his best as a GN section hand for many years and had earned the right to a less physical assignment.

President John Budd in Saint Paul would have approved of this no-nonsense guy. Vito always waved at passing train crews, but with a demeanor that implied he wanted us off his crossing quickly. We were a nuisance and kept him from much more important things to do, such as safely moving autos and trucks over *his* crossing.

A railroad sideswipe collision occurred adjacent to Seattle's Galer Street. Vito's on-the-spot view of the accident made him a star witness. His testimony would be crucial in determining fault. He received a notice to be present at the investigation.

The official opened the inquiry and noted the crossing watchman's absence. All present agreed to proceed while awaiting Vito's arrival.

Vito thought differently. He'd not vacate his post or trust another to handle the job. No sir! Vito vetoed that plan. He belonged on *his* crossing.

All other testimony had been heard and the group recessed. Others were on the phone and searching for Vito. They found him at his regular post, secured a replacement, and shanghaied him. The fellow had crucial information.

A belligerent crossing watchman entered the room, stared at the two tape recorders with their octopus-looking microphone cords, and glowered at all present.

The official cajoled Vito into divulging the needed personal data such as full name, age, occupation, length of service, etc. Vito endured the rest of the routine questions. An official then asked, "Did you see the passenger locomotive approaching on the main line?"

Vito gave a scornful look and replied, "Yaas."

"Did you then see the switch engine with cars approaching the crossing?"

"Yaas."

"Were you of the opinion a collision was imminent?"

"What's dat?"

"I shall rephrase the question. The passenger engine was coming towards you as the switch engine with cars moved to the main line. Did you believe either one would stop short of an impact?"

"What's dat you saying?"

"I'll try again. The passenger engine is coming down the main line, and the switch engine with cars is over the crossing and moving to the main line. Did you think the passenger engine would hit the boxcars, like this?" (He raised both arms and drove the right fist into the left palm.)

That did it! Vito replied, "Oh! Why you no say dat? She'sa com'a down da track, she'sa stop, she'sa no stop. How da hell I know?"

The official asked the key witness to remain seated while he clarified a point for the record. Railroad timecard direction at Galer Street differed from compass direction.

That fact might confuse others, who would read the investigation transcript. The ten-minute explanation made clear that north and south were east and west for railroad operational purposes.

"And now, Vito," he continued. "With that point made clear, please tell us, on which side of the tracks were you standing when the accident occurred?"

Vito appeared astounded. Didn't everyone already know his answer to that question? He proudly poked a finger to his chest and replied. "I'ma onna mya side."

Lack of evidence avoided one investigation. The incident involved two extra gang foremen, two motor cars, and one big collision. They met on a curve. There were no injuries, but much embarrassment and worry over one demolished motor car.

Two culprits plus a derrick operator conferred. With *clam shell* attached to the boom cables they did what had to be done and buried the debris . . . er . . . ah . . . evidence.

One fact that could not be ignored. Most hogheads rarely sat and squirmed through an investigation. But when disciplined, it came second to the anguish and hurt pride. I believe officials understood that.

Chapter Six
Changes Galore

Diesel-electric power had infiltrated yard service on the Great Northern's Cascade Division as early as 1939. In the mid–1940s they came streamlined and with tattletale speed tapes. Management averred, "We couldn't afford to keep going with steam engines. Too much maintenance, and they pound hell out of the tracks."

The P-2 class 2500 steam locomotives dominated passenger train service for decades. Could they be replaced? It appeared Engineer Al White, a 1908 hire, and Fireman Bill Murphy, a 1941 engineman, started the trend when they accompanied the 2507 into Puget Sound. A massive slide caught *Number 27*, the westbound fast mail. It dumped the engine over the stone block seawall at a point between Everett and Seattle. Fireman Bill sustained the only injury. He lost part of one thumb that early February morning in 1948.

Some may have considered the injury as not serious, but two *complete* thumbs held upward by a railroader

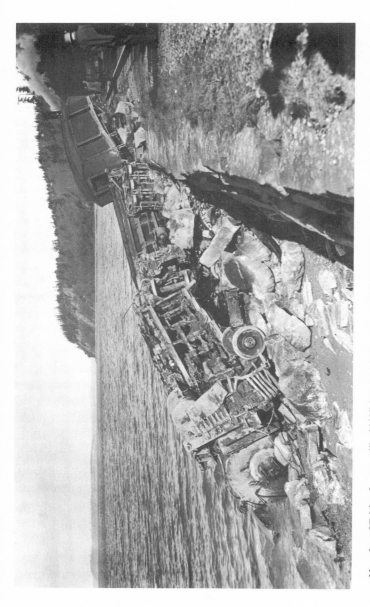

Number 27 (the fast mail), Al White, engineer, and W. P. "Bill" Murphy,fireman, February 18, 1948, 5:30 A.M. (Note the scar from another slide just west of the point.)

meant, "Let's go eat or go home." Not being able to give that important sign, Bill surely had a disability.

Another *first class train*, one with diesel power, took a similar plunge in 1961. Engineer Pat Burns, a 1916 hire, and Fireman Mel Rake, a 1955 hire, rode the *Empire Builder's* engine into Puget Sound at high tide. Pat, helpless with a broken shoulder, may well have drowned had Mel not kept his head above water until help arrived. One typical get-well card read, "Hi, Pat. We heard you joined the navy."

Meanwhile, the P-2 steam prima donnas languished in the roundhouse. Their cluttered cabs served as lunchrooms for employees. One did time in work train service only because it came equipped with a *booster*. The occasional stint hauling the varnish, for which they had been built, helped delay their fate. Those trips happened only during a shortage of diesel power.

Harry Geerds, a 1902 hire, worked in passenger service between Seattle and Portland. He planned to retire soon and had quickly adapted to new diesel, two-unit consists. He liked 'em. In fact it irked Harry when on occasion the roundhouse fired up and trotted out an old 2500 for his run south.

Harry devised a plan. When the phone rang he'd immediately ask the crew caller, "What kind of power ya got for me this morning?" If advised a steam engine, Harry laid off and went back to sleep.

We envied a person who could turn down a passenger run to Portland on any type of iron horse and chided Harry about his elite status. He shrugged off our comments with, "I'm too damn old to be bounced around for one hundred and eighty miles each way on one of those rib-bruisers."

New road diesel locomotives did not cause a job-loss scare as had the historic completion of the Cascade Tunnel, line change, and seventy-four miles of electrification. Complacency set in. Diesels be damned, they couldn't hurt us! Exhaust fumes in the big tunnel demanded that even the new streamlined *Empire Builder* must have an electric helper between Skykomish and Wenatchee.

The two new *Bull Mooses* held title as the largest single unit electric locomotives in the world. Surely the GN wouldn't buy them if they intended to *smoke* diesels through the big bore. We'd have bet on that. But management had plans, and they didn't include seventy-four miles of trolley wire.

Pete Tenerelli, a veteran Skykomish section crew member, had the same opinion. Electrics didn't impress him either. He'd been oiling switches on the back lead near the roundhouse and stared at the giant 5018. I invited Pete to climb up and have a look around.

He showed no emotion as we toured through the power plant. I boasted, "Why this one electric unit can do more work than two Mallets and . . ." We returned to the cab where Pete took a final look at the controls, especially the new type seats with arm and back rests. I asked, "What do you think of her, Pete?"

My exuberance hadn't swayed him. He shrugged his shoulders and replied, "She'sa all same barbershop; da chairs go round and round."

The officialdom in Saint Paul, Minnesota, had made their decision. Nostalgia hadn't set in yet when the last steam engine puffed out of Seattle on March 24, 1953—or on July 31, 1956, when the one remaining Bull Moose, GE 5018, towed the last three Westinghouses east on their final trip for Cascade Division electric locomotives.

GN 5018, Wenatchee, Washington, June 9, 1956. *Courtesy of Warren W. Wing.*

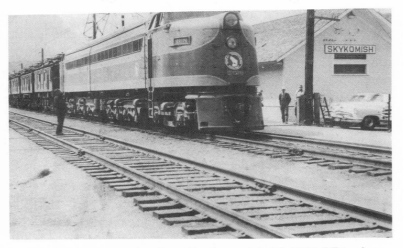

Last electric run on the Great Northern, July 31, 1956, GE towing Westinghouse. Left Skykomish 1:20 P.M., arrived Wenatchee 5 P.M. Andy Strom, engineer; Sonny Cleveland, fireman.

Engineer Rudy Hany commented after only three trips in helper service with a four unit freight diesel. "By golly! That's the first time in thirty-five years that I could set a cup of coffee in front of me while the engine moved."

Electrical Superintendent Joe Gaynor became a lone dissident. His parting shot came after I'd notified the dispatcher by radio that one of the four diesel units had malfunctioned, and we'd have too much tonnage for the 2.2 percent grade. Joe cut in loud and clear with the message: "Put pantographs on the roof of that thing and it'll work OK."

Others worried that diesel powered locomotives would overheat in the tunnel and shut down—and they did. The trailing units required oxygen, but instead received mostly exhaust from the lead units. If the train stalled on the uphill side in the tunnel, because of a chimneylike effect; all previously accumulated exhaust flowed past crew members before it exited the tunnel's east portal. Respirators, issued to employees and placed in *refugee bays* along the tunnel wall, failed to supply complete safety.

Ingenuity, trial-and-error, plus sage advice allowed the GN to continue the use of diesel power through the "big bore." A tan house, constructed at the east portal, forced fresh air into the tunnel and past oncoming engines. It also "flushed" the residual exhaust after a train exited.

A huge metal door closed and sealed the east portal as the next eastbound freight train entered at the west end. The closed door at the upper end and the moving train created a piston-in-a-pump situation. It produced considerable pressure against the door and made a seventeen mph speed restriction mandatory for most freight trains.

Even so, ears popped when the pressure released with a bang as the big door opened. Bauxite ore had begun to move east in big *hoppergons* to an aluminum refining plant. This created yet another hurdle, which plagued management. The sudden pressure release caused the bauxite to spew from supposedly airtight cars. The fine but gritty ore piled up alongside the rails. Passing trains swirled it around, causing damage to equipment.

The ever-inquisitive hoghead, R. J. "Bob" Smith and his son Jim, an engineman since 1965, made an observation of the problem from two vantage points—their work place on the locomotive in hill freight service, and from the ground while at their family's summer cabin on Nason Creek near the east portal.

Larger cars moving in some trains restricteded the free flow of air to a greater degree. The pressure build-up forced air into the supposedly airtight bauxite cars. When the tunnel door opened suddenly, the release of pressure allowed the gray white ore to be blown out of the cars.

Small spring-loaded and louvered vents in the tunnel's big door solved the problem. Instead of the pressure being released explosively when the big door opened, it was allowed to dissipate gradually. The modified system worked, solving the bauxite escape problem.

A new era had begun. Railroad radio communication allowed fewer people to move more tonnage. At first we disliked that chatter-box attached to the control stand. Noise aplenty already prevailed in the locomotive cab. But some loved it—we called them "radio-active."

Radio communication made for a more efficient operation. It also included a dozen or so additional rules in the *Book of Rules*. Conversations could be monitored by both the railroad and the Federal Communication Commission.

A bunch of close-knit railroaders, working together night and day, occasionally lapsed into informal voice identification instead of the required official procedure.

The need for proper train identification became apparent one day during a stop at a station on the east slope. Two freight trains, each with diesel helper units cut in the middle, met there. They'd been ordered to swap helper engines at that point. Three engineers and one conductor answered to the name "George." The brakeman's *walkie-talkie* transmitted loud and clear, "Back 'er up, George." Luckily no one responded.

Profanity headed the taboo list. One such violation occurred in the Rocky Mountains east of Whitefish, Montana. The freight train conductor, busy at his desk with waybills, looked out of a caboose window into the darkness. He'd failed to find a familiar landmark to determine location. Grabbing the radio handset he blurted, "Hey, Bill, where 'n' hell are we? I'm all screwed up."

Before the engineer could reply, another voice cut in, "Great Northern Railway Trainmaster Fisher in GN auto calling the person who has just transmitted. Identify yourself immediately!"

After a long pause Fisher received his answer: "I'm screwed up, but not that screwed up."

I intended it to be a prank! But it exemplified the true merit of railroad radio. We'd eased down the westbound main line at Mukilteo and the brakeman dropped off the engine near a section gang on a *spur track*. He'd make a cut behind forty-five cars—twenty of them to be shoved into a storage yard. The locomotive stopped around a curve and out of sight. The routine procedure normally required three brakemen in order to relay hand signals to the engineer.

But this train came radio equipped. An amazed section foreman, unaware of the new method for passing signals, stood beside the locomotive. He'd watched, mystified, while we completed switching, and coupled our train together.

"I ain't never seen a hoghead do that before," he said.

I replied, "Do what? You mean set out a cut of tank cars? You're kidding me."

"Naw, I know damn well you couldn't see anybody around that curve. How'd ya know when to stop, go ahead, stop, pull out of there, and shove back to a joint on your train?"

"Oh, that. Well some things ya gotta know to run an engine; the other guys will learn when they've been around a bit more."

A few trips later he shook his fist as I passed him. He'd been informed, and knew I'd been assisted by another "new gadget."

Radio communication stopped upon entering the Cascade Tunnel, because of lost airwave continuity. But we needed it because of another innovation: "Radio Controlled Locomotive Equipment." We called them "slave units," and operated them remotely from a console placed in the cab next to the control stand. The system demanded unbroken radio signals to power units in the middle or immediately ahead of the caboose. Installing a transmission cable the full length of the tunnel solved that problem.

Remote-controlled locomotives proved to be not feasible, at least in the mountainous area. The decision came as a relief; I'd often worried about the reliability of operating distant units that anybody could climb aboard and mess around with.

The system required absolutely careful predeparture brake tests, because both locomotive consists could pump air into the train line. One preparatory test made sure that the control unit's air-brake supply had reached the caboose unassisted by the remote unit's compressors. One of the tests assured us of that.

We'd coupled to our westbound train one morning and began charging the train line brake system prior to testing. I radioed the caboose, gave our train and engine number, and inquired, "Is the air coming up on your gauge?"

The rear brakeman answered, "Nope, not here it ain't."

"You should have it showing now. Will you check the *angle cocks* on the caboose and a few cars to make sure? The *swing brakeman* is on his way back and also checking the train line."

"OK."

Thirty minutes later the swing man announced, "I'm on the caboose, we have a full charge, it's a tight train line, and you can set 'em up for a brake test."

"OK, but why the problem?"

"Well, I'm in our caboose on track seven, and the rear brakeman is waiting for the air to show on the gauge in a caboose on a train on track nine."

Remote control made me nervous—especially in mountain territory. I knew about those sudden surprise downhill speed accelerations, and I feared 'em.

Block signals existed on all main line routes long before I became a railroader. Connecting them to a new *slide fence* protection device was an innovation that came during my time on the GN. Trains often stopped because of rocks or animals activating the slide fence warning. I disliked those delays, but I knew there'd be a time when a slide fence or block signal might save my life. Five such occasions remain vivid memories.

One occurred on a late Sunday night during a rainstorm, and shortly after we'd departed Skykomish westbound with a drag. Moisture from the head brakeman's wet rain gear had fogged the windows after he entered the locomotive cab. The three of us reached for paper towels to clear the windshield and proceeded on an expected *straight shot* to Interbay.

The first omen came by way of the yellow and then a red CTC signal just eight miles out of Skykomish at the town of Baring. After we stopped, the dispatcher gave us an OK to proceed at restricted speed, using a routine procedure. We stopped for yet another signal. After rounding the next curve, the next signal glowed a pretty green one half mile ahead. The applicable rule required the entire train to pass it before increasing to normal speed.

Two wet rails glimmered in the headlight's beam, but did not continue to the clear signal. Why? More paper towels swabbed that windshield as we reduced speed to less than ten mph and inched closer to the dark spot. Someone hollered, "There ain't no railroad there!" He spoke the truth; a massive slide had moved it forty feet down a steep bank and into the raging south fork of the Skykomish River. Four locomotive units and three guys surely would have been down there were it not for modern safety devices and the rule book's definition of restricted speed: "Proceed prepared to stop short of train, engine, obstruction, or switch not properly lined, looking out for broken rail *or anything that may cause the speed of a train or engine to be reduced*, but not to exceed twenty mph."

Another instance saw us departing Seattle for Vancouver, B.C., on Amtrak *Number 794*. I blew my special whistle

Check List - R.C.L

Continuity Test
Whenever train separated
or stopped where an angle
cock could be turned——

1. Notify caboose you are
   going to test & receive O.K.
2. Cut out brake valve
3. Turn mode selector to M.U.
4. " feed valve sw. to in.
5. Notify caboose of release.
6. Pull A.B.R. button, note
   feed valve lite on.
7. Caboose O.K.s a brake pipe
   increase.
8. Watch for a brake pipe
   increase of 5 p.s.i. or more.
9. Cut in brake valve.

a pinched air hose & continuity
loss, together! — pray

MEMO

Brake Test

1. Press A.B.A. button until a 15 p.s.i. reduction made.
2. When exhaust closes turn feed valve sw. to out.
3. Turn mode selector to isolate.
4. Cut out brake valve.
5. Wait 40 seconds for equalization.
6. Observe leakage.
7. Press A.B.A. button to get E. reservoir pressure below brake pipe, (not over 3 p.s.i.)
8. Cut in brake valve.
9. Complete full service brake pipe reduction.
10. Cut out brake valve until test completed.

signal as our train came up on Bridge 4, five miles out of the depot, and only one hundred and fifty yards from home. At that point I used the locomotive horn to say, "Hi, we're on our way; see ya tomorrow afternoon."

This trip turned out to be different than expected. We'd traveled another three miles when a block signal turned from green, to yellow, to red only seconds before we passed it. There had to be a reason. We stopped and then sneaked around a curve. A large tree spanned both main lines as it slowly twisted in an ugly mass of oozing mud. I shuddered. What if we'd been seconds earlier, or there'd not been a slide fence to activate the signal?

The radio allowed us to warn other trains and notify the dispatcher, who had us back our train down the eastbound main line into the depot. That move created another problem: what whistle signal shall I use as we crossed Bridge 4 again and so soon? Interpreted it should mean: "Hi, a real fast trip, huh?" It's wonderful when good luck keeps a hoghead high, dry, and out of rivers or Puget Sound! Those new gadgets and old rules also deserved credit.

Drag lights began to appear along main line routes, and were soon followed by scanners that stood as sentinels at various points and scrutinized passing trains for defects. The information appeared on a display sign ahead of the engine. Radar guns also abounded during this new era, but then others could clock a train's speed from the dispatcher's office.

New, more powerful diesel locomotives replaced those that started the many changes. They might have astonished old-time hogheads. Water coolers replaced the gallon jug that sat on the cab floor. Locomotives hauled more tonnage, and they had flush toilets, too! How appropriate, for soon women would become train crew members.

CTC or Centralized Traffic Control soon followed. The standard twenty-one-jewel watch, a timecard, a batch of train orders and some judgment would no longer determine where, when, and how trains met or passed each other. The dispatcher in Seattle pressed buttons and lined the routes for us. He, or she, truly told us where to *head in*. Through-freight brakemen in CTC territory no longer needed to unlock and hand throw passing track switches. The many innovations contributed to a future job loss for their craft.

Officials considered one particular dispatcher to be an expert CTC person. He agreed with their assessment and wanted to keep it that way. But he irked many freight hogheads working the east end. They'd slow down and then stop a full-tonnage train because of an unnecessary red signal. The delay included time spent recharging the brake system, which when added to the start and acceleration cost them many minutes.

Call it "pouring salt on the wound." Immediately after each delay, his voice came in loud and clear, "All right extra west at Gold Bar, you've got that block, now let's gitta-gittin.' " If we hadn't come to a complete stop, but had to do so in order to release and recharge, there'd be the question, "What's holding you up? Let's get a move on."

We'd reply, "If you hadn't stopped six thousand tons in the first place this train would be fifteen miles closer to the terminal." No reply—he'd gone off the air before the rebuttal. There had to be a reason. Why sure! That's it! He transmitted those gung ho words for the recording tape. Others, hearing his authoritative voice, assumed that train delayer to be a great expediter.

Later, an edict ordered CTC dispatchers to ride locomotives on their district at least once a year. I found my

First remote control board in Cascade Division, forerunner of CTC. *The Seattle Times.*

former nemesis in the cab with grip and gloves one afternoon. He saw CTC signals as they appeared to us—around
curves and on ascending or descending grades. We became
friends and went to dinner together upon arrival and tie-
up in Wenatchee. Both of us had a common goal—*keeping
our tail out of the gate.* But he had the advantage—all those
buttons on that console. He could stop full-tonnage trains
with a keyboard and one finger.

Why feud when more important things abounded?
There'd been scuttlebutt; the GN might merge with three
other lines. Some said, "Yeah, they tried that way back in
1931 and Uncle Sam sidetracked 'em."

Meanwhile, labor unions, people in that other Washington, and possibly a changed management attitude
brought forth protection for employees adversely affected.

The long overdue maximum allowable duty hours in
any twenty-four hour period became a serious topic. Nego-
ciations resulted in a gradually reduced maximum hours
of service from sixteen to fourteen to twelve. We also wel-
comed and enjoyed vacations with pay.

Sporadic strikes, wage increases, and contract rule
changes appeared to be necessary in the era following
World War Two. I'd noticed an interesting fact regarding
pay raises; it never failed! Each time the newspapers carried
an item of a wage-rules controversy settlement, our hotel
room rent increased accordingly. Ditto for restaurant ham
and eggs. At long last that happy day arrived when our
employer picked up the lodging tab and a small part of our
meal costs.

President Eisenhower and Postmaster General Sum-
merfield struck a blow with the edict, "RPO cars must go.
Mail will be transported by truck and airplane." Loss of
the mail contract eventually scuttled passenger trains on

STANDARD BASIC DAILY WAGE RATES
FOR
LOCOMOTIVE ENGINEERS
ON
RAILROADS IN THE UNITED STATES
EFFECTIVE DECEMBER 16, 1953

Weight on Drivers (Pounds)	Through Freight	Local and Way Freight	Passenger	Belt Line, Transfer and Yard Service
Less than 100,000	$15.73	$16.25	$14.82	$16.89
100,000 to 140,000	15.73	16.25	14.91	16.89
140,000 to 170,000	16.16	16.68	14.99	17.32
170,000 to 200,000	16.16	16.68	15.08	17.32
200,000 to 250,000	16.33	16.85	15.17	17.49
250,000 to 300,000	16.48	17.00	15.25	17.64
300,000 to 350,000	16.63	17.15	15.34	17.79
350,000 to 400,000	16.84	17.36	15.42	18.00
400,000 to 450,000	17.05	17.57	15.51	18.21
450,000 to 500,000	17.26	17.78	15.60	18.42
500,000 to 550,000	17.47	17.99	15.68	18.63
550,000 to 600,000	17.65	18.17	15.77	18.81
600,000 to 650,000	17.83	18.35	15.85	18.99
650,000 to 700,000	18.01	18.53	15.94	19.17
700,000 to 750,000	18.19	18.71	16.02	19.35
750,000 to 800,000	18.37	18.89	16.11	19.53
800,000 to 850,000	18.55	19.07	16.19	19.71
850,000 to 900,000	18.73	19.25	16.28	19.89
900,000 to 950,000	18.91	19.43	16.36	20.07
950,000 to 1,000,000	19.09	19.61	16.45	20.25
Over 1,000,000	Add 18¢ For Each 50,000 pounds	Add 18¢ For Each 50,000 pounds	Add 8¢ & 9¢ alternately for each 50,000 pounds	Add 18¢ For Each 50,000 pounds

the GN. We'd hoped to work those runs before retirement. But we hardly had time to bemoan that loss when top echelon people of four major railroads filed another petition to merge in 1961. This one might succeed.

Many employees adopted a "so what" attitude. Others knew of mergers already in effect, but mostly between short-line and terminal companies. History indicated railroads had become giants by acquisition or consolidation. Our plight might be different if the Great Northern merged into a 25,000-mile conglomerate.

In 1965, a group of us sat in a steamy Oakland, California, hotel meeting room and listened carefully while an expert explained the situation before and after mergers to a bunch of hogheads. Our mentor, L. S. "Pete" Loomis, from the Brotherhood of Locomotive Engineers, did his best considering there'd be a boxcar load of legal papers before our paychecks and timetables read Burlington Northern instead of Great Northern.

It became a reality as of March 10, 1970. One disgruntled employee mumbled, "They should've named it the Burlington Southern—those initials on the rolling stock best described the new company."

The *dovetailing* of seniority rosters had been a dilemma. But a guaranteed earning clause, plus swallowing pride over rights to hold better runs, saw us become payroll numbers on a railroad giant. We kidded each other in locker rooms, and referred to the other guy as a "brand X hoghead."

Streamlined locomotives be damned! Blunt-nosed brutes, with more than twice the power of earlier diesels, sat on the roundhouse tracks. Even the main line tracks didn't clickity-clack anymore because of continuous rails.

Management, physicists, metallurgists, civil, electrical and mechanical engineers combined to make it happen. It had to be that way—other transportation modes had sneaked up on the railroads.

Chapter Seven
A Moving Workplace

There'd been another change! It too sneaked up on us. The people I. E. Clary had once referred to as "those kids" now held the better jobs, and they talked at length about how it used to be.

The new old-timers begrudgingly admitted, "Those youngsters move trains pretty damn well. But they'd been paid for student training and hadn't kept a full head of steam on a Mallet, while looking around its boiler to see the track ahead. Nor had they worked a sixteen-hour day. . . ."

But then our predecessors had referred to us as "guys who hadn't shoveled tons of coal into greedy locomotive fireboxes, cleaned a fire, or felt a hot cinder down their necks. . . ." Did these younger hogheads have a similarity? Yes, when they studied seniority rosters as we had done. They, too, eagerly awaited *our* retirement, while we reminisced about about the past.

A perch, ten feet above two ribbons of steel, had given us insight other than just operational changes on the GN / BN. I felt fortunate to have had an opportunity to spend forty years on a job with a moving workplace. Many beautiful, unforgettable, and sometimes strange sights crowded into my memory bank.

Historic Skykomish supplied more than its share of remembrances. A daytime view included numerous mountains and the confluence of several small rivers. My job also meant many night runs. We saw the Northern Lights dancing over the top of Beckler Peak on clear October/November nights, while we waited to cut in our helper locomotives.

An unforgettable meteorite shower viewed from the west end of town above Bare Mountain took first prize. It surpassed all Fourth of July displays I'd ever witnessed. The phenomenal display appeared to be so close; we'd wondered: Might some of the burned-out residue strike the locomotive cab roof?

Popping out of the west portal of the eight-mile tunnel at Scenic on clear cold January nights served as yet another plus for nights runs through the Cascade Mountains. The Tye River glimmered as the snow on tree branches sparkled in the moonlight. If only an artist could have captured such scenery! Others, working day jobs, missed out on the unparalleled beauty of the valley in the dead of winter.

A highway snowplow's flashing yellow light, far below, indicated others also worked those hours. Both the state highway employees below and train crews on the mountainside appreciated another advantage that accompanied the serene setting—much too cold for slides, washouts, or avalanches.

Both Bear and Bare Mountains augmented the beauty of the Skykomish area on day trips, but a real bear surprised me. The big black brute appeared inebriated! I saw its teeth as it glared at me from a distance of only twenty

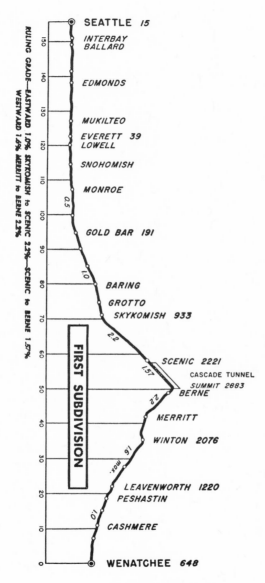

East end track profile.

feet! The monster sat and swayed back and forth atop a pile of corn.

The event occurred at a rock alcove alongside the track between the towns of Scenic and Skykomish. A bulldozer had shoved the contents of a derailed hoppergon car loaded with corn into the place on the cliff side. The car needed to be unloaded in order to rerail it. A rainstorm plus a week of July sunshine produced liquor. Yup, fermented right there at the base of Tonga Ridge!

Because of the accident, a train order restricted our speed to ten miles per hour while passing that natural distillery. We'd rounded a curve, and I reached to close the cab window to avoid the stench, but, my God! The gigantic animal considered our train an intrusion. It glared at me and then scooped up more of the hootch. I stared in amazement as the excess spilled from its mouth—that critter was drunk!

How could I be so sure? Well, I'd seen many black bears and their cubs near the railroad tracks, but never face-to-face. The bark of a steam engine, the whine of electric motors, or the roar of diesel units turned 'em around; they'd scamper away. I mostly saw their other end. This bruin showed defiance as it rocked back and forth atop the mound. He sat where the drinks were on the house, and he intended to remain seated.

The ever-changing panorama also included some eyesores. Mother Nature had made numerous land alterations long before man arrived. But railroad builders, timber barons, and highway constructors defaced much of the landscape over a relatively short period of time. Most of the ravages happened long before my group came upon the scene. We witnessed some of the recovery, but noticed a few new scars. The healing in progress appeared evident.

Most of the denuded land lay in areas not suited for farms, cities, or homes.

A Great Northern line change in more recent years served as an example of how a despoiled land bounced back. One plot of a heavy-equipment-rutted quagmire stood out for all to see. Rivulets of muddy water laced the area in fall and winter. Dust blew from the barren soil the next summer.

One didn't need to be an environmentalist to appreciate the way the trackside area healed without intensive care. Common weeds soon covered the scarred land. A decade passed. Vine maple and alder trees dominated. They served as soil enrichers for the Christmas-tree-sized fir, cedar, and hemlock.

Hill crews noted the beauty of deciduous trees in the fall. They created a wonderful sight, especially on the east slope of the Cascades. People drove from all points to see, paint, and photograph the autumn variety of colors displayed by the leaves of maple, birch, and aspen. We admired the sight from across the Nason Creek canyon and State Highway 2. But at times the fallen leaves blew across the canyon and landed on the tracks!

We needed all the traction available when westbound on the hill with a full tonnage train. Pesky aspen leaves might cause us to stall or break into. The bright yellow menaces soared like birds, and, as if by automatic pilot, landed on the rails. Even the ones that touched down and were blown away left a dime-size splotch of lubricant. A train crushing those that remained compounded a spinning-wheels problem. I remember trips when the speed dropped to a low of six miles per hour.

With *sanders* on and the diesel electric's amperage gauge pointer far *into the red*, we'd struggled along. On two occasions, when about to give up, Brakeman Norm Francis came to our rescue. He grabbed a broom and rushed ahead of the near-stalled train, while sweeping leaves from the rails. When the engine *found 'er feet* and speed increased, I'd whistle-signaled to let him know he'd saved our day. People might not believe a one hundred and fifty pound man with a broom kept a six thousand ton train moving on a 2.2 percent uphill grade.

Railroaders on a desert or prairie division covered more mileage in less time than those of us working on coastal or mountain divisions. The Cascade Range provided a barrier, which milked incoming rain clouds from the Pacific Ocean. It changed our runs east in both landscape and climate. We'd leave the mountain goat's domain soon after clearing the Big Tunnel.

Pine trees decorated the less jagged terrain. Farmland prevailed as we crossed the Wenatchee River and exited the Chumstick Tunnel. A sweeping curve at the tunnel's east end enabled crew members to *eyeball* the entire train, checking it for a hot box or sticking brakes. I remembered the big curve best with electric locomotives on cold winter nights. Both the head end and the helper's pantagraphs arced as they slid along the iced-up high-voltage trolley wire. The brilliant flashes momentarily illuminated homes, farmland, and trees. The spectacular sight gave warning: "Be careful around high voltage."

Several miles more and in the spring we noted apple and pear orchards in bloom. Peaches, apricots, and cherry trees soon joined the group. They all depended on the Wenatchee River, which scurried alongside on its way to join the mighty Columbia. The GN hauled much of the apple harvest to market, and the big river gobbled up more tributaries as it assumed a greater power and irrigation task.

From the same area we saw the brow of a distant hill; it denoted the exact center of Washington State.

Trackside landmark familiarity played an important part while working in coastal fog or mountain snowstorms. The powerful locomotive headlight reflected off that white stuff, while hogheads anxiously sought block signal indications. Nevertheless, from *clam digger* to *apple knocker* country on the *other side of the hill*, I liked that run.

The east side required warmer clothing in winter. But night runs, daytime heat, and a steamy Wenatchee hotel room in summer deglamorized the job a bit. An open window, a hoped for breeze, and our own five-dollar portable fan helped as we sought needed sleep. At times our competition, the cross-country trucks, appeared to seek revenge. They roared by on the street below as we tossed and turned in an attempt to be rested for the night trip back to Seattle.

On one occasion a radio blared all day from down the hall in the old hotel. That night while *registering* out at the yard office, my conductor asked, "Did you have a good sleep?"

He'd asked the wrong question for I replied, "Hell, no! Some jackass had a radio turned up all day long. I heard soap operas for six hours. Let's see, I listened to, 'As the World Turns', 'All My Children' . . ." It appeared I'd forgotten some for the, now sheepish, conductor filled in with the others and hurriedly headed for the depot.

Better hotel rooms—and air conditioned, too! They were a blessing for away-from-home railroaders. Seniority presented an alternative. If dissatisfied we might bid on and move to another run; the one to Portland, Oregon, for instance. But it also had advantages and drawbacks. A typical locker room conversation concerning such a change might be, "Ya like blowing a whistle for one hundred and eighty miles and worrying about the guy in the gray Chevrolet, who ducks across in front of ya? How about the nut in the tan station wagon talking to his wife, who doesn't know he damned near got hit. The three scared kids in the back seat knew."

The first forty-five miles between Interbay and Tacoma stood out as a whistle blower's paradise. One got lots of practice there. Upon leaving Tacoma and skirting southern Puget Sound, we went inland through farm and timber country for many miles. and there she wandered again—an even mightier Columbia River had taken another route. She now served as a gateway for oceangoing ships. Some flew a foreign flag and had names we couldn't pronounce.

These important transportation systems and the rubber-tired giants that roared along nearby on Interstate Highway 5 depicted freight transportation U.S.A. An aerial photograph at that point might sell a lot of calendars. Lest I forget, trains on that run hauled airplane fuselages for a not-so-little company named Boeing.

We'd later compete for right-of-way with ships at bridges spanning both the Columbia and Willamette Rivers near Portland. A crew, whom had already been delayed several times en route by other trains, often waited for those ocean-going transporters below. Tired and hungry railroaders then discussed bridge tenders and favoritism. "Show me a delayed hoghead who doesn't complain and I'll show you a sick railroader."

The Seattle to Vancouver, B.C., trips also had an abundance of road crossings and competed with boat traffic at bridges. I remember one trip where I might have blown a long and hearty whistle signal, but didn't. The incident occurred while crossing a bridge over the great Fraser River and into New Westminster. They both served as a backdrop for a most unusual stage setting. Our seat in a locomotive cab most surely qualified as being in the choice loge section. It began the afternoon of July 14, 1959, at the Interbay roundhouse in Seattle. The *head brakeman* boarded the engine with more than the usual clearance plus train orders. We kidded about the abundance of information. I asked, "What's in this catalogue ya handed me?" We'd been called to work *Number 712*, a freight run to Vancouver, B.C. Two long pages of instructions, dated back to July 8, advised of Queen Elizabeth's tour across Canada. Thirty-five GN Cascade Division officials and employees plus three train crews received the edict: *"The Royal Train MUST NOT BE DELAYED!"* An additional wire message directive for *our* train read: "EVERETT AND DELTA ARE LINED UP TO HAVE YOUR PICKUP READY SO YOU CAN GET RITE OUT AND MAKE NEW WESTMINSTER BY 3:00 AM OR AS SOON AFTER AS POSSIBLE TO CLEAR FOR ROYAL TRAIN."

We also received order number 403 that night at Blaine, the border city. It read: "EXTRA CN 6519 LEAVING NEW WESTMIN-STER ON WEDNESDAY, JULY 15TH RUN AS FOLLOWS WITH RIGHT OVER ALL TRAINS. . . ." No doubt about it: Woe be unto a crew who *sticks* that CN hot shot.

But why all the fuss? The schedule for Canadian National *Special Train Extra 6519* had it not coming onto the bridge and GN track at Fraser River Junction until 8:00 A.M. Our crew planned to be bedded down in a Vancouver hotel much earlier.

I wondered about the required five mile per hour speed limit over the bridge. Must Extra CN 6519 also slow to that speed? If so, had the welcome committee considered Her Magesty's daylight view of the industrial area near the outlet of the big river? Old lumber, tin cans, bottles, rusted oil drums, and other jetsam littered the dirty sand beach across the river from beautiful New Westminster. Surely

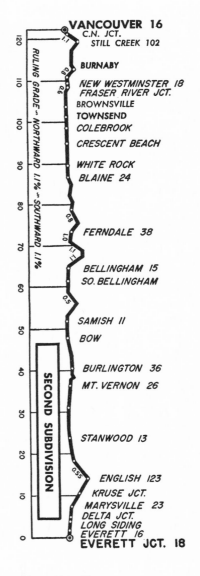

VANCOUVER 16
C.N. JCT.
STILL CREEK 102

BURNABY

NEW WESTMINSTER 18
FRASER RIVER JCT.
BROWNSVILLE
TOWNSEND
COLEBROOK

CRESCENT BEACH

WHITE ROCK
BLAINE 24

FERNDALE 38

BELLINGHAM 15
SO. BELLINGHAM

SAMISH 11

BOW

BURLINGTON 36
MT. VERNON 26

STANWOOD 13

ENGLISH 123
KRUSE JCT.
MARYSVILLE 23
DELTA JCT.
LONG SIDING
EVERETT 16
EVERETT JCT. 18

RULING GRADE ~ NORTHWARD 1.1% ~ SOUTHWARD 1.1%

SECOND SUBDIVISION

CASCADE DIVISION 1966

Everett to Vancouver.

not an appealing sight for the royal entourage. We'd over-looked the ingenious Canadians; they had the situation well in hand.

Our train eased around the curved trestle into Fraser River Junction and onto the long span at 3:15 A.M. Surprise! The drab area ahead and below, illuminated by floodlights, appeared light as day. Numerous mounted police in dress uniform strolled the grounds. I shouted across the cab, "There's lawn, flowers, and trees down there—it's a park! Come look at this. Pullman cars sit on a new track . . . a staircase and walkway lead to the water's edge!"

I'd been blowing the engine's whistle for one hundred and forty miles, but certainly not here and at this hour. We'd have awakened the Queen. The beautiful fairyland below appeared as if it had always been there. Extra CN 6519's *right over order* allowed for a delay without speci-fying a place. It became clear: those in charge intended the site to be secret, serene, and splendid.

All of us on that GN freight train eagerly awaited the return trip that afternoon—there'd be another look at that masterful landscaping job. Surprise again. As if it all had been a mirage, only a deserted dirty-sand beach remained. A tree branch, a piece of lumber, and a lone empty beer bottle bobbed offshore, where beauty had been a few hours earlier.

Thirty-one years later, on my last trip before retire-ment, I looked down from an Amtrak engine at the beach below Fraser River Junction. I remembered Her Majesty's visit and the work skilled landscapers delivered and then took away.

I considered the north end, with Vancouver, B.C., as its distant terminal, a good run. But it, too, had some draw-backs. Many trains shared the double track, twenty-eight miles along Puget Sound, with pedestrians. They enjoyed the beach, but often worried train crews. Our warning whistle might only move them to the other track and in front of a train going the opposite direction. Another hurrah for railroad radios. They allowed crew members to warn other trains of people on their track. Educational programs explained the danger to school children. It certainly helped as did overhead foot bridges.

A few trespassers hid in the bushes on the bank side and practiced rifle shooting or rock-throwing at locomotives and cabooses. I'd had two locomotive windshields broken in front of me. Radio warnings, special agents on the prowl, and bulletproof glass alleviated that problem.

Brakeman Don Reiling's ordeal, along with many others, no doubt prompted the protective innovations. Don was on a hill run, scanning his train from the caboose, when he took a near-fatal shot in the chest. The bullet continued barely missing Conductor Ken Woite.

The woman who stopped her auto and blocked both main lines at the Edmonds ferry dock crossing had an alibi for her misdeed. She said, "Now who would think they ran trains on these tracks?"

After leaving the industrial area of Everett, we passed some of the country's best farmland. Next came another look at Puget Sound sprinkled with the San Juan Islands. The setting sun beyond the islands dazzled tourists on Amtrak's northbound run. I used "old sol" and Lummi Island to check my watch on midsummer trips. The precise amount of sun showing above the island assured me of an OK timepiece and an on-time arrival at Bellingham, the next stop.

T.W. Mackenroth
E. Khatain
E.H. Nelson
C.H. Moreau
} Seattle

11-10-70

At about 12⁵⁰ a.m. date train 88
Extra 6414 East Engr George Leu
when passing a point about 1/4 mile
west of Carkeek Park someone threw a
rock breaking windshield on engine
6414. Engr. Leu suffered facial cuts.

D.A. Stuart
Condr.

Turkey Trail describes some of the GN trackage north of the border. That fact is authenticated by a conversation with an official from another railroad. He rode with us on an Amtrak locomotive north to Vancouver. We cleared the border stations of Blaine and White Rock and whistled past Colebrook, B.C. Our guest pointed to the left in the darkening sky and asked, "What's that bright light over there?"

"Oh, that's Grouse Mountain, a ski resort and restaurant."

Five minutes later came the question, "Well, then what's this next light up there on our right side?"

"It's the same light."

Another ten minutes upon leaving New Westminster, the light appeared directly ahead. It caused the query, "Are you sure you guys know where you're going?"

Our group had worked turkey trails, *drag strips, snake paths, back alleys,* the hill, *midnight goats,* the Annie, the Upriver Job, work trains, and Amtrak. General roundhouse Foreman Bill Blum once doubted my sobriety after one of those trips. He rushed out of his office waving my work report. An item on it read, "Replace broken cab-window glass and inspect electrical components for damage due to high seas." (A high tide and wind collaborated to send huge waves crashing over the stone seawall along Puget Sound.) I doubted if many hogheads had run a locomotive through high seas. But there'd been those two engine crews who rode engines into Puget Sound. Others had been saved from swims in the rivers.

We'd also operated steam, electric, and diesel locomotives with away-from-home terminals in two states and in Canada. The time had come to think about a last arrival on a roundhouse track and first day of retirement. What would

I tell my many grandchildren and hoped-for great-grandchildren should they ask, "What's a hoghead, Grampa?"

I'd explain, but they must hear of their long-since-departed great-grandmother's reaction when a railroader said, "I know your son. He's hoghead, isn't he?"

The word puzzled my mother, but she handled the question easily and replied, "W-e-ll, even as a young boy at home he could be very pig-headed at times."

Chapter Eight
Retirees

"Pig-headed" or not, the occupation suited me. Most of us expected it to be interesting, a challenge, and not without a few drawbacks. I'd been on the Great Northern's payroll about three years when the Road Foreman of Engines, John Ferrell Jr., handed me a letter he'd received from the superintendent's office. The letter appeared to be a job application. It stated, "I have watched trains pass by my home, and I believe I'd enjoy driving one of those locomotives. However, and before accepting employment, your railroad must meet certain work conditions:

"1. All work to be between the hours of eight and five.
"2. Absolutely no work on Saturday, Sunday, or holidays.
"3. All trips must originate and terminate at my town.

"If these conditions can be met, please advise when I should report to your office."

Young locomotive enginemen considered the letter to be sincere but humorous. With those stipulations, the applicant may still be waiting for a notification. One of them might possibly have been met, but only after thirty years of seniority.

During our low-seniority days an attorney challenged my being selected as a juror in an auto-accident case.

He asked, "What is your occupation?"

I replied, "Engine service, Great Northern Railroad."

"Oh! That's similar to being in the army, isn't it?"

"I don't think so."

"You do have a book with many rules that must be strictly obeyed. Isn't that correct?"

"Yes, sir."

"And that's the same as with a soldier, is it not?"

"Yes, sir; but if unhappy with my job, I can quit, and I believe a soldier had better not do that."

A few new hires did not accept irregular hours, extra boards, and lots of night work. They *pulled the pin* before gaining seniority and rights to better assignments. For those who stayed to retirement—I've yet to hear a switchman, train or engineman say, "I wish I'd quit that job much sooner."

Retirement and the last run fanfare reminded me of earlier days when school dismissed and summer vacations began: sleeping in, swimming, baseball, picnics, or just doing nothing.

Doing nothing! Not these guys. After forty years of railroading, it appeared they wanted another interesting activity. One of our predecessors had vowed upon retiring, "I intend to occupy a comfortable rocking chair. On days when I feel real good, I'll rock faster." His rocking chair remained in excellent condition, but our early-day mentor didn't. His departure served as an admonition: "Find other endeavors."

R. J. "Bob" Smith set a good example. A rocking chair was not for him. He continued his interest in railroads by doing volunteer consultant work as a hobby. Bob also had a problem, or was it his three sons who had the dilemma? They claimed, "Dad wants to remodel our houses, whether they need it or not."

Norm Nicklen, another 1940 hire, also had a number of pursuits. World War Two interrupted his early railroad career. Norm did Marine Corps duty in the South Pacific.

Upon his railroad retirement, he practiced cabinetmaking and other hobbies, such as commercial fishing. Then came the big endeavor, the one we believed he'd never finish—violins! Not as a virtuoso—retired GN Conductor Orville Hostteter had that job *sewed up*. Norm, after much study and finding a rare book by the old master himself, constructed not one, but two violins.

Amateurish? The University of Washington's School of Music didn't think so. Nor did Orville, a graduate of that school and a veteran violinist, who played in two well-known symphony orchestras. He classified Norm's violin as superior. The highlight for us other retirees came at a regular luncheon meeting of former Cascade Division railroaders. Retired Conductor Orville, using Norm's violin, entertained the group with well-known tunes.

This collaboration between the two GN / BN railroaders had an interesting twist. Norm's father, Engineer George Nicklen, had been a veteran Great Northern 1916 hire. Orville's Dad, of the same era, had been a veteran Northern Pacific conductor.

We'd started out as a divergent group of young guys, banded together by an industry: a railroad watch, timecard, rule book, and two ribbons of steel. We retired, scattered, and became diversified once more. Most had other skills and hobbies.

What have I done? Well, er, ah, violins appeared too tough, but I did build a fence around my garden, traveled, looked at locomotives of other nations, attended writing class, and continue to hike in a nearby park three times a week. That reminds me: while this old retired *throttle jockey* puffed along on one of those hikes, an attractive, young lady jogger passed me on the trail. She stopped, pointed to the Great Northern logo on my cap, and said, "Are you a railroader?"

"Yusta be."

"What did you do?"

"They called me a hoghead. Oh, guess I should explain. . . ."

"You don't need to because that's what I am on the Burlington Northern."

Several months passed and I met Nancy again. She jogged with a partner, another attractive young lady. Nancy introduced her as a freight conductor on the Portland run.

OK, OK, but mademoiselles hadn't run Mallets.

Epilogue

The book has dwelt mostly on Great Northern Railway enginemen. I concentrated on that craft because I knew it best. Certainly we were not alone out there.

The mainland United States is tied together by railroads which cross, trans-crisscross, and run parallel over our entire continent. A multitude of people kept trains running, while only the train and its crew were visible each day. One last anecdote, my favorite, makes that point.

Train dispatchers played an important role in the everyday operation of railroads. But on this day, Tony, a section gang foreman out in the boondocks, outranked everybody and proved it.

Tony's crew maintained the trackage in a remote area. He'd check in at the nearest depot each morning and receive the latest lineup of trains and their expected arrival time at his location. Should he need more information he relied on a wayside company phone system. It required a certain protocol. One unlocked the shanty, positioned a small knife switch, and listened. If a clear line, the caller pressed the send button and said, "Dispatcher," and gave his location, occupation, and name. He then waited until he was acknowledged. The dispatcher handled the calls in order of their importance.

Tony knew that what he had to say that morning superseded all others. But he didn't say so! He'd cut into a conversation with a loud, "Allo, Dispatch, disa Tony!"

The busy dispatcher, occupied with putting out train orders, replied, "Tony, I'm busy."

Tony continued to shout, "Allo! Allo! Dispatch!"

"Dammit, Tony, I'm busy! Get off the line!"

"Allo! Allo! Dispatch!"

The now-irate dispatcher reached towards the switchboard and unplugged Tony's line. Five minutes later, having completed the task at hand, he connected to Tony's line and heard the familiar, but weakened, "Allo, allo, dispatch."

There came a break. Tony released the send button, and the dispatcher said, "Y-e-a-h, Tony, what is it?"

"Dersa biga-biga rock—shesa come down da hill. Boom! Shesa stop between da rails and blocka da track. You hell of a busy guy, Dispatch, but yousa donna know where tis—good-bye."

"What did you say? Hello, Tony! Come in, Tony! —Oh, Jesus. . . .''

Glossary

Do we really need to translate railroad jargon? This anecdote is an answer to that question. A group of Chinese exchange students attended the University of Washington in Seattle. They had a fair command of the English language and, among other subjects, planned a study of American industry. What better place than a railroad? A few became switchmen at Interbay Yard and soon began to understand the lingo.

Switch Foreman Tom Tapping thought he'd given a simple order when he pointed and told one student, "Run around those *gondolas* and shove 'em to a joint on track seven."

The fellow headed that way but returned to ask, "Is not a 'gondola' an Italian boat?"

A
Aggregate. Total hours worked are not continuous but "split shifts" that must be within one twenty-four hour period.
Air bench. A section of the roundhouse specializing in air-brake equipment maintenance and repair.
Air gap. The trolley continuity is broken and the two wires run parallel to each other. This allows sections to be shut down for repairs.
Angle cock. Air brakeline valve on each end of cars in train.

Annie job. Annacortes local freight run.

Appleyard. Two miles east of Wenatchee.

Apple knocker. One residing east of the Cascade Mountains.

Automatic block signal. Activated by engine or cars.

B

Back alleys. Tracks servicing downtown warehouses.

Back into. Correct or disagree; argue a point.

Back lead. A yard track from which other tracks diverge.

Beans. Breakfast, lunch, or dinner.

Bid in or on. New or vacated job assignments awarded according to the seniority of aspirants.

Big Tunnel. Eight-mile bore between Scenic and Berne.

Big wheel. Contained the steel blades of rotary plow.

Big wing. A part of the snowdozer, which could be moved out and braced for clearing a large area. Generally used to clear more space for additional expected snowfall.

Block signal. Indicator of track ahead—semaphore and/or colored lights.

Boiler head. The part of the boiler directly in front of crew, which forms the front wall of the engine cab; the valves, levers, and gauges are located there.

Boomer. See **Springboard.**

Booster. A small steam engine under the cab and geared to drive the trailer truck wheels.

Break into. Accidental separation of cars or engine because of failed or broken equipment.

Bull Moose. Man in charge, i.e., boss. Also one of the latest electric locomotives: 5018 or 5019.

Butt burner. Investigation, "hearing," bawling out.

By train order. Notified by a typed or written instruction.

C

Caboose cushion. Black durable mat for bunk.

Clam digger. Resided west of the Cascade Mountains.

Clam shell. Attached to cables and handled by a derrick to move large amounts of materials.

Clear shot. No stops to the terminal or other location.

Clearance. Train's authority to occupy the main line.

Color at the stack. The exhaust smoke, or another way to check combustion.

Coupler. The apparatus that connects cars or locomotives to make up a train. See **knuckle, pin, drawbar, pinlifter.**

Crossover. Switches and trackage to move train or engine from one set of tracks to another.

Cut-in. Couple up additional helper locomotives, or open an air supply valve for braking system.

Cut of cars. A group of railroad cars that are unattached to engine or caboose.

Cut-out. Train separated, allowing helper engine to move to a side track.

Cylinder cocks. Mechanisms to release condensed steam.

D

Dead head. Ride the train as a passenger

Double cab. Two power units.

Double-head. When a helper engineer's power is placed ahead of the train's regular engine.

Double track. Two main lines, trains may meet or pass without using a passing track.

Dovetailing. Fit into combined seniority rosters according to original hiring date.

Drag. Slow freight train—not a highball.

Drag light. A warning device activated by dragging equipment.

Drag strip. If inclined to exceed posted speed, do it here.

Drawbar. The heavy basic part of the coupler.

Drop. Uncouple moving car or cars behind the engine.

Dump the air. Apply brakes in emergency application.

E

Extra board. A substitute or unassigned service.

Eyeball. Scrutinize a moving train for defects. See **roll by the train.**

F

Field excitation. A process used in electified zone. It allowed the engineer to regulate resistence, harness, and return energy to substation. Main purpose: downhill braking.

Firebox. Combustion area of steam boiler.

Firetube. Type of boiler, as opposed to watertube.

First class train. Generally passenger service, as on employee's timecard, trains are superior by right, class or direction, right is conferred by a train order.

Flyer. Passenger train.

Found 'er feet. Regained traction.

Full head of steam. Maximum boiler pressure.

Full service. Maximum air-brake application short of the emergency position.

Fusee. A flare.

G

Goat. Switch engine.

Gondola. Steel open top car for moving bulk material.

Gorilla cage. Caboose.

Grab-irons. Stationary bars to assist when boarding eqipment.

Graduate the release. Release brakes in increments in such a manner as to prevent a lurch while bringing (especially a passenger train) to a complete stop.

Grease cellar. A prepacked metal container, which when in place, became a spring-fed lubricator for steam locomotive driver wheel axles.

Guide cups. Filled with engine oil, not valve oil. They could be adjusted to lubricate at a desired rate.

H

Half a glass of water. Normal level of water in boiler as shown by gauge glasses—Very important.

Head brakeman. Generally rode the engine.

Head end. Front of train or the locomotive, ie., "head end crew."

Head in. Enter side track to pass or meet another train.

Helper. An additional engine and crew for steep grades.

Highball, highballers. Fast, speedy (applied to trains); an engineer; or a hand signal to depart.

Highcar. A self-prepelled repair shop to maintain the trolley wire.

Highwheeler. Passenger train locomotive.

Hill. Mountain area.

Hoghead. Locomotive engineer.

Hooked up. To shorten valve stroke as speed increases. Could be likened to shifting gears.

Hoop. A bamboo or plastic rod with a loop on one end used to hand up orders to moving trains.

Hoppergon. A covered gondola-type car, which unloaded from the bottom.

Hostler. At locomotive service points this person moved engines as required.

Hot as a firecracker. Steam pressure and water levels gauges as they should be.

Hot box. Overheated axle on car in train.

Hot cable. The one we feared with 11,500 volts.

Hot shot. Very important train.

I

Into the red. High-end zone of an amperage gauge—a warning.

J

Joint track. Used by more than one railroad.

Juiced. When a person is burned by high voltage.

K

Keeping tail out of gate. Staying out of trouble.

Kicked out. Shut down by circuit breaker action.

Knuckle. See **coupler** and **pin**. The part of coupler that swivels and locks in place to make connection between cars and / or locomotive.

L

Lead. A track from which other tracks branch from.
Light engine. Engine only.
Line the switch. To move a lever that changed route.
Lined up. Position track switches.
Little black book. Consolidated Code of Operating Rules. Also called the *Book of Rules*.
Long overcoats. People who made trackside tests for possible rule violations.

M

Maintenance of way flags. Approach warning and / or stop signals because of track repairs ahead.
Mallet. Locomotive with two engines. Both are supplied steam from one boiler.
Marker lights. On cabooses. Shows red to the rear when train occupies main line; one shows green when on the siding.
Mark up. Take an open job other than by bid.
Maximum permissable speed. As specified by sign posts and in ''special instructions.''
Meter charts. A record of kilowatts used on a trip.
Midnight goat. Third shift switch engine.

O

Oil boy. Person who supplied each outgoing engine with necessary lubricants, ie., valve oil, engine oil, engine oiler, wool waste, fusees, jug of drinking water, etc.
Oiled around. Using a spouted hand oiler to lubricate engine parts from the ground level.
Old head. Senior employee.
On the ball. On time, good job, etc.
On the bricks. Fired; furloughed; etc.
On the fly. Without stopping.
On the point. On the head engine consist.
Other side of the hill. East or west of the Cascade Mountains.
Overload kickout. Result the same as **lost the wire**. One is at the substation curcuit braker jacks and the other on the locomotive.

P

Pantograph. A cantenary type connection between electric locomotive and the overhead wire.

Picking up. Adding cars to train while en route.

Pick up an old man with a crate of eggs. A very slow speed.

Pilot beam. The large heavy steel bar across the front of steam engines.

Pilot conductor. Required by contract rules on all main line movements.

Pin. A round, heavy steel rod, which holds knuckle to coupler When lifted by a lever, the knuckle can swivel or be removed.

Pin lifter. The rod and handle used to lift the pin allowing the knuckle to open and uncouple the car.

Pool freight. A group of men each taking his turn to unassigned service.

Pull the pin. Uncouple engine or cars; quit; retire; etc.

R

Rail auto. Automobile equipped with flanged wheels enabling it to run on rails.

Refugee bays. Spaced openings in the tunnel's side wall.

Regeneration. Regenerative braking. Braking with electric locomotives.

Register. A large book in which both conducter and engineer must enter all pertinent trip information.

Rerailed. Put back on the track.

Right over order. Made a superior by train order instead of by class.

Roll into braking. Set levers in advance and allow increasing speed to change from power to braking.

Roll the train by. Visual inspection of a moving train from the ground by a person on the ground.

Roundhouse. A circular building for servicing locomotives.

Run light. Engine only.

Runner. Locomotive engineer.

S

Sanders. Small pipes and nozzles that blow sand on rails ahead of wheels for better traction.

Service application. The normal air brake application—not emergency.

Set out. Place cars from train onto another track; deliver.

Sewed up. As a job or run already occupied by a senior **hoghead** or one who could not be bumped.

Short flag. Not the prescribed distance from danger zone.

Shuffling boxcars. Switching; moving cars to different tracks.

Shunting. Moving cars from one track to another.

Side track. Track adjacent to the main line providing a byway for meeting or passing of trains.

Siding. See **side track.**

Skipper. Conductor.

Slide fence. A heavy wire mesh fence connected to the block system. When struck by a sizeable object, it gave advance warning.

Smoke box. The forward part of the boiler drum, where exhaust from each side join before exiting out the smoke stack.

Smoke through. Work steam or diesel engine through a tunnel.

Snake path. Track with many curves.

Snow king. The one in charge of snow removal crew or crews.

Spotfire. Just enough fuel to maintain steam pressure while on standby.

Spotted, spot-up. To place engine, cars, equipment in an exact position.

Springboard. To move often from job to job; the person also known as a **boomer.**

Spur track. Open on one end only; dead-end track.

Stack. Smoke stack; the outlet from the smoke box.

Sticks. Stuck; delayed.

Straight shot. No stops.

Swap power. Exchange locomotives as steam to electric or vice versa.

Swing brakeman. Liaison between conductor and other brakeman.

Switch. A lever to move engine or cars from one track to another.

T
Tacked on. Coupled.
Tail track. A short section of straight track such as at a **wye**.
Take 'er bumps and come on line. To synchronize with power source in electrified territory.
Take the blanket off. Run engine (iron horse) at full throttle.
Taking water. Filling the water section of locomotive tender.
Tank hook. Long steel rod used to reach and pull water spouts over the tender.
Tank top. Top of locomotive tender.
Tender. A part of the steam engine which held the fuel and water.
Throttle jockey. Locomotive engineer; a **hoghead**.
Tie-up. End of run or shift.
Torpedoes. Explosive devices placed on rail and activated by wheels of engine or train to give a warning noise.
Triple cab. Three units operating as one.
Turkey trail. Many curves; branch line; **snake path**.
Turn. Position as in **pool freight** or unassigned service; first in, first out; they must be called in their turn.
Turnaround. Returned to starting point before reaching distant terminals.
Two-two. 2.2 percent mountain grade maximum allowable grade for main line class one railroads in the United States.
Two unit Westinghouse. The number and type of units in the locomotive consist.

V
"Vanderbilt" tank. A more modern tender tank for steam engines.
Varnish. A passenger train.

W
Washout signal. Violent stop signal meaning extreme danger.
Waybill. Data pertaining to a car in the train; document with details of shipment.

Whistled out a flag. Engineer signals the caboose to protect rear of train.

Wooden axle. Old style, ancient, run-down.

Work grip. A usually beat-up looking traveling bag used to carry a copy of the *Book of Rules*, time cards, rain gear, shaving kit, thermos bottle, etc.

Work train. Nonrevenue maintenance or snowplow service.

Wound up. Fast, as with a locomotive.

Wye. A Y-shaped track layout for turning equipment where turntables are not available.

Y

Young runners. Recently promoted to engineer.